# The Call Heard
# 'Round the World

# The Call Heard 'Round the World

Voice Over Internet Protocol and
the Quest for Convergence

DAVID GREENBLATT

## AMACOM

American Management Association

New York • Atlanta • Brussels • Chicago • Mexico City • San Francisco
Shanghai • Tokyo • Toronto • Washington, D.C.

Special discounts on bulk quantities of AMACOM books are available to corporations, professional associations, and other organizations. For details, contact Special Sales Department, AMACOM, a division of American Management Association, 1601 Broadway, New York, NY 10019.
Tel.: 212-903-8316. Fax: 212-903-8083.
Web site: www.amacombooks.org

*This publication is designed to provide accurate and authoritative information in regard to the subject matter covered. It is sold with the understanding that the publisher is not engaged in rendering legal, accounting, or other professional service. If legal advice or other expert assistance is required, the services of a competent professional person should be sought.*

*Library of Congress Cataloging-in-Publication Data*

Greenblatt, David.
    The call heard 'round the world : Voice over Internet Protocol and the quest for convergence / David Greenblatt.
      p.  cm.
    Includes bibliographical references and index.
    ISBN 0-8144-0752-8
    1. Internet telephony.   2. Convergence (Telecommunication)   I. Title.

TK5105.8865.G74 2003
004.6—dc21

                                    2003001035

*Printing number*

10  9  8  7  6  5  4  3  2  1

To my wonderful family, and to the Chairman of IDT, Howard Jonas, together with the many hard-working executives and employees of IDT, IDT Telecom, IDT Media, Net2Phone, and Winstar IDT Solutions. Without your inspiration, guidance, support, and friendship, this book would not have been possible.

"What is mine, is yours. . . ."

# Contents

Preface ix

Introduction xiii

**CHAPTER 1**
You *Can* Get There from Here:
The Promise of Convergence 1

**CHAPTER 2**
Two Hot Dogs with Mustard: Our Humble
Beginnings 15

**CHAPTER 3**
Selling the Dream 31

**CHAPTER 4**
The New World of Communications:
The Market's Perspective 47

**CHAPTER 5**
The Power of Convergence: The Industry's
Perspective 71

**CHAPTER 6**
The Red Pill or the Blue? Ways Your World Has
Changed 89

**CHAPTER 7**
"Someone Will Be There Between Nine and
Five . . .": Broadband/Cable 113

**CHAPTER 8**
Lions, Tigers, and Bears: The Powers Behind
Convergent Services                                    129

Epilogue                                               151

Appendix A: Glossary                                   153

Appendix B: Abbreviations and Acronyms                 171

Bibliography                                           173

Index                                                  175

# Preface

As the title of this book suggests, Voice Over Internet Protocol (VoIP) and Internet Protocol (IP) telephony are communications phenomena with worldwide impact. This solution has dramatically enhanced phone services, Internet and multimedia capabilities, and broadband cable offerings, resulting in more seamless communication and better integration of sight and sound unhindered by regional or technological boundaries.

*The Call Heard 'Round the World* imparts my vision for a world that is only a *local* phone call away and is not dictated by a particular device or limited to a single type of communication. VoIP has created a means of sharing information using sight and sound over any number of devices—phone, computer, television, handhelds—you name it. Beneath these offerings, there exists a network so strong, flexible, and intelligent that communications happens effortlessly on a global basis.

As chief operating officer of Net2Phone, I helped our team of pioneers to develop advances in VoIP and conceptualize the types of services we could provide that would alter how consumers and businesses share information. Net2-Phone now serves more than 40 percent of the retail IP telephony market. As the CEO of Adir Technologies, I again have assisted in bringing the vision of "local connectivity" to life.

Everyone involved in our team, as well as our vendors and partners, shared a belief that VoIP held the key to the future of communications convergence.

I am proud of the effort we made in bringing VoIP to consumers, businesses, and investors looking to strengthen their own communications efforts, business models, and portfolios. In this book, I am pleased to be able to finally share the story of what it was like bringing VoIP to the world stage. *The Call Heard 'Round the World* chronicles this journey and provides an in-depth look at where our lives as consumers, business professionals, and financiers will be over the next few years as the worlds of data, communications, and media converge.

Divided into eight chapters plus an Introduction and an Epilogue, the book tells the story of convergence and VoIP, describing how the convergence market was identified and cultivated. In addition to citing cases from Net2Phone and Adir, examples from established players are offered throughout the book. Where appropriate, I have also included business and financial data to help readers quantify the potential of convergence, and VoIP services and technologies.

The book's early chapters explain the role of Net2Phone and Adir in developing convergent solutions and services. They then describe the VoIP marketplace both from an industry and from a market perspective. Chapter 1 describes the potential for convergence for consumers, business users, and those in the telecommunications industry, clarifying and defining what makes up convergent services and the role VoIP has taken in driving advances in communications. The next chapter traces the roots of VoIP to Howard Jonas, founder of IDT and later Net2Phone, who is a pioneer and visionary in the field of telecommunications. IDT has emerged as a telecommunications powerhouse responsible for revolutionizing the industry through a number of innovative products and services, the most recent being VoIP. Adir Technologies, a spin-off of Net2Phone, licenses and further develops the VoIP technology originally created by Net2-Phone. This chapter is filled with colorful characters and intriguing power plays in Adir's history. Chapter 3 traces our journey spreading the word of VoIP around the world.

Moving into specifics about VoIP, Chapter 4 explains the opportunities convergence from a market perspective. Investors, managers, and media professionals interested in this emerging market will find this chapter valuable. It provides definitions, market statistics, and examples of how VoIP is currently playing out within the worlds of business and finance. Chapter 5 looks at the role VoIP has assumed within the telecommunications industry. Besides consumers and business users, the services that make up VoIP and convergence are being sold primarily through large telecommunications carriers. For companies like Adir, the telcos represent the main customers. This chapter provides more detailed technical and financial information for managers of telecommunications and cable companies looking to include convergent services in their portfolio of offerings.

But what fascinates me the most is the way convergence has enhanced services available to users worldwide both at work and at home. Chapter 6 overviews the main categories of convergent services being offered right now, with specific information about market interest and revenue potential as well as brief examples of those companies most active in each area. Chapter 7 looks at how broadband cable has brought convergence and IP telephony more fully into the home. Cable users number in the millions; delivering services over cable dramatically increases the number of homes that use and benefit from communications convergence and adds richer service delivery to the devices used to carry such services.

Chapter 7 explains in detail the reason that cable has emerged as an important driver in VoIP, the market potential for IP cable going forward, and the ways the telcos and media companies are partnering to grab onto this lucrative market.

An important chapter for industry types, Chapter 8 features cases of the industry's most prominent players by sector: technology and service. Companies cited include equipment vendors, service providers, and system integrators including Nortel, Alcatel, Cisco, Net2Phone, and ITXC.

The book's epilogue looks at how convergence is preparing to take communications, cable, and media into the future within the context of the current economy and volatility in the telecommunications industry. As businesses and financiers rebound from a depressed market and the negative repercussions from the collapse of such firms as Global Crossing, convergence remains a beacon of hope for those committed to the potential of communications technologies and services.

# Introduction

There are as many ways to interpret what the term "convergence" means as there are theories on how it will transform communications. Convergence describes the melding of video, voice, and data and the sharing of that information over devices that are connected to an IP network. Communicating seems fairly straightforward, but as the ability to create richer content becomes a reality, there is a real desire for instant and convenient access.

I'm compelled to write this book because I am witnessing the merging of technologies and services that we have come to accept as isolated and independent of each other. The ability to add voice to communications that were previously data intensive—online transactions, email, financial reports—is upon us. There is a clear and immediate need for human interaction in all forms of communication.

I firmly believe that convergence and the way in which it will change how we communicate is the result of technological superiority, market readiness, and perfect timing. The union of these elements will herald a new era in communications.

The devices we use today to access and share information—the telephone, the Web, and television—will take on an entirely new and innovative form once aligned, becoming more powerful in their scope and use. By combining an Internet Protocol (IP) network with the intelligence of Voice Over IP (VoIP) solutions, convergence will allow the devices we use to work together as an integrated and interactive whole. VoIP is synonymous with IP telephony because it allows for the connection of several complex technologies. The ways in which it can be used are virtually limitless. VoIP makes convergence possible. .

The goal of convergence is to achieve widespread connectivity through a single device. We currently define the PC, the TV, and the telephone as having certain parameters, but convergence will make these devices interchangeable. The kind of data that can be transmitted in real time will be unlimited. The backbone of convergence is IP networks—wide-open platforms that can accommodate "packet" transmissions. The packet can include combinations of voice, text, video, and/or audio. High-bandwidth IP can compress data and allow for multiple transmissions over the same line—whether it is wireless, landline, or cable. IP networks can be combined with intelligent solutions to create smart devices and services designed to provide seamless, natural, and meaningful communication. As you read this book, you will discover just how IP networks through convergence form a "new world" of communications that allows for the combination of visual, textual, and audible information.

Combining advanced connectivity with intelligent network solutions will result in content that is more compelling and methods of communication that are more satisfying. No longer will consumers submit to mechanized service that is restrained by bandwidth and platform. Consumer offerings will become much more gripping as voice and data converge.

With convergence, you can use your digital television to conduct transactions right from your living room, accessing an actual human being who will personalize your experience and complete the transaction. Consider what this means for consumer businesses—how it could revolutionize sales for products sold through infomercials and shopping networks. For noncommodity ecommerce companies, adding a human voice to the customer experience will become essential. In addition to retail, we are going to see the impact of convergence on industries that hold content at their core: financial services, health care, insurance, media, entertainment, publishing, and advertising.

Consumers may well come to expect a rich, multifunctional relationship, making it difficult for companies to sell their products and services or distribute information online without a "live" component. IP telephony is revolutionizing the interactive experience by bringing in an actual person to handle online encounters seamlessly, naturally, and in real time. Ultimately, consumers will have a richer relationship with the companies that they deal with.

Imagine if you walked into Nordstrom's—one of the best places in the world to shop, a brand built on the promise of excellent customer service—and there was no one there to help you. You'd leave, wouldn't you? The same holds true for Web interactions. Right now, the Web is like Nordstrom's with no employees.

Ask yourself why instant messaging has become so pervasive—and what this type of connectivity could do for etailers or econsultants? In fact, if you apply a live component to any site—publishing, health care, self-help, community resources—the impact it would have on an individual's life is staggering, and the value this type of service would bring to a business, incalculable. And isn't it the promise of value that Wall Street rewards?

The creation of Net2Phone was a signal event in the industry. It at once communicated the value of VoIP solutions in the telephony marketplace—introduced two years ahead of competitors—and at the same time foreshadowed the strategies and trends that companies in telecommunications, the Internet, and the media are now implementing. As these industries meld, the transformation they will experience will be nothing short of a rebirth driven by the ability to create and deliver content in unlimited ways. Mergers between distribution and content companies are one indication of this shift. Net2Phone adds human interaction to all types of Web communication—whether it is instant messaging, personalized communications, or conducting purchases from a host of digital devices. Although the cost-effective nature of IP technology is the key to market penetration and the creation of more profitable services, cheap phone calls are not what it is all about. Improving the means by which we communicate is the true goal of convergence. This ability is one we believe will impact lives, personally and professionally, across the globe.

In this book, I hope to share with you the excitement of championing something that will positively impact people worldwide, and offer a glimpse of the world to come. A new age of communications is upon us—one that can't be forecast or predicted or budgeted for. And that's what drives my colleagues and me. Bringing convergence to the world stage has been my role for as long as I can remember—even before I joined Net2Phone in 1999 as its COO. A little later in the book, I describe for you the pace and palpable excitement of this time, the continuing influence of Net2Phone and IDT, and the types of relationships and strategies that took what some thought of as a pipe dream to profitability. My greatest desire as you read this book is for you to open up your imagination to the richness of information you will be able to access through convergence and the myriad ways in which we will share it in the future. Along the way, you will come to understand the modern world of communications—its acronyms, key players, and bankable technologies—and you will begin to envision the future of communication.

What will the services that we will come to use in our professional and personal lives look like? How will we benefit from them? How can you employ convergent thinking and services in your own business? How far can we take IP telephony, and who will be its champions in the future? Whether you are reading this book as a service provider, manager, investor, or interested consumer, the answers to these questions will be revealed to you in the chapters ahead.

# The Call Heard 'Round the World

# CHAPTER ONE

# You *Can* Get There from Here:

## The Promise of Convergence

Whether by divine intent, serendipity, or strategic design, I have consistently found myself being a champion for Internet communications technologies. Earlier in my career, I worked at Nextwave (now Veracast), an early Internet startup. I was the senior VP for research and development for the company's most promising ConferenceCenter™ products. The product I designed delivered real-time presentations over the Internet. The viewer would see a live speaker in one panel and have the ability to interact with the speaker by typing in questions. The speaker's dashboard provided various surveying and interactive capabilities. Investment banks sponsor investor technical conferences at hotels around the United States. We offered these seminars live over the Internet; they were also recorded in multiple formats for later viewing. This might seem like pretty simple stuff now, but this was in 1995 and 1996, the early days of the Internet and internetworking. Although Internet video technology was barely working, I began to understand and develop a vision for what is now called "convergence."

While functionality and dependability are taken for granted today in networking, during this period at Nextwave we were never quite sure whether the technology was going to work. Delivering live communications was truly the "bleeding edge." Even though the technology at the time was less robust than our vision, those of us who worked on the ConferenceCenter project had witnessed the impact of live delivery on the communications experience. This capability resonated with the users, too; they had a richer encounter in real time. Once we saw this positive reaction, we got even more creative with the interactive capabilities of our product. But, it was primarily our team's ability to see past the blemishes of a new technology and to find ways around that technology's limitations that fueled our vision of convergence. The Nextwave experience bolstered my commitment to the idea of IP convergence, as well as the commitment of those who worked with me at Net2Phone. Even though there were a lot of gaps that needed addressing in order to bring high-quality interactive communications to the marketplace, no one saw them as a real deterrent.

The reason I have been such a strong advocate for IP voice technology and have served as an industry spokesperson for convergence is that I feel it is worthwhile to invest in the quality of our communications. Our emotional and mental health are very much determined by how we communicate. The methods by which we communicate impact how well the information we convey is understood. We are affected, molded, and impacted by our communications all the time. Convergence has the ability to make communication richer and more meaningful and then to deliver it around the world. In essence, who we are, what we are, and how we make it through life are molded and defined by how we communicate.

> Communication involves connotation, interpretation, and analysis—it's what the data *mean*. Good communication means that the data means more.

It's true that technology makes communication happen at a utilitarian level; but its psychological and sociological impact is dramatic. My efforts are not about getting things faster, quicker, or cheaper or about advancing a particular technology as a means in and of itself. It's not about computers replacing adding machines. Rich, geography-independent communication cables deliver the full vibrancy of information—anytime, anyplace, anywhere. This impacts who and what we are, what we *think* we can do and what we actually *do*.

> Most technological advantages focus on improving a single tool. Communication is not just a tool that we use; it is a reflection of an individual as a whole person. It's the platform for everything we send to and receive from the world around us.

## In Search of True Convergence

Convergence is a term that has come into vogue recently, and there are many interpretations of just what "true" convergence is. In its essence, convergence refers to the transmission of data, voice, and video over a single network, often in combination to provide richer services. In the past, different types of networks were needed to manage different types of communications, so voice went over one network and data went over another. This is no longer the case. Today the running of "converged media" over an IP network is reliable and economical and can grow (or scale) with the user's needs. Network convergence, digital convergence, and communications convergence— are general terms for the same thing. My belief and that of my peers is that convergence will shape and enhance how individuals and organizations share information. Internet audio, video, animation, and instant communications flowing over one network instantaneously create a new platform for communications that will change both how we conduct business and how we handle our personal communications.

The primary way consumers will access converged Internet communications at home will be through a broadband network. With convergent technologies traveling over IP networks, consumers will have access to a plethora of new services. The same services that corporate users enjoy— advanced messaging, Web talk, voice portals—are easily extended to individuals at home. Consider the technologies that we view as commodities: personal computers, email, voice mail, speech recognition, and even the Internet. Each of these began in academia or in business enterprises. Today, it's hard to find a consumer who doesn't have one or more of these technologies at home. Cable, wireless, television, PCs, PDAs—these are the technologies of the consumer, and they can each accommodate convergent services. Enabling Web sites with voice interaction capabilities is one example of voice portal services that allow the user to actually speak with a site representative. In 2005, it is estimated that more than two billion people will use Internet voice portals, voice-enabled Web sites, and other Web-enabled voice systems.[1] (Voice portals and other convergent services are covered in greater detail in Chapter 6.)

Now that the connectivity is in place and convergence is on the horizon, it is up to smart managers and investors to rethink their traditional methods of conducting business. Ironically, almost everyone, from CEOs to Wall Street investors to the analysts, agrees that no one can predict the type of services that will be born of convergence. Almost anything is possible. But the applications that emerge will have to meet market needs when the market is ready for them.

> The confluence of timing and technological advances is what determines what will succeed. Great technological advances often fail because the timing was not right.

The introduction of important communications technologies—IP networks, VoIP solutions, advanced networking, cable technologies, and new ways of thinking about distributing content—is part of the confluence of events that will engender true convergence. The essence of this new paradigm is a piece of technology called the softswitch, which replaces the circuit switch technology used in our public switch telephone networks (PSTNs). I examine the technology more in Chapters 3 and 4.

The softswitch is widely considered "the Holy Grail of telecommunications,"[2] offering complete interoperability, enhanced services, user self-provisioning, and flexible billing, all in one service. The National Convergence Alliance estimates that the worldwide softswitch market will reach $5.7 billion by 2004.[3] Technology companies like Cisco, 3Com, and others are targeting carriers and service providers as their primary markets. But it is also the vision of these companies to influence the types of services being offered to consumers and enterprises.

> "Convergence is not a question of is, it's a question of when. The full definition we don't even know; technology has changed drastically. Just several years ago, few enterprises were using email and no one was using the Web."

—Mordy Rothberg, Chief Strategy Officer, Adir
Technologies

Complete interoperability makes it possible for any type of data on any type of device to be transmitted to some destination regardless of the device or networking technologies being used. IP is the great unifier for integrating technologies. It permits "self-provisioning," a fancy industry term for the options open to users who can do everything for themselves. They can customize their messaging services by using tools such as subscriber control, enhancing and making more productive their work and home lives. With self-provisioning, the user can ensure access to voice and email messages from one number, anywhere in the world. Self-provisioning also includes access to special features and services via the Web, a PDA, or some other wireless device. With self-provisioning, users can specify what features they want to use and how, and where and when these features will be used. Some simple examples of how communications will change are priority ring lists, onetime setup for conference calls, and time-based call forwarding.

So, convergence is more than the ability to transmit voice, video, and data over one network. It involves the convergence of tools and devices, as well, and the ability to do the same things in the voice world that you do in the data world and vice versa. Because convergence involves data, entertainment, and voice, the cable market is likely where true convergence will happen, since that is where the necessary bandwidth and capabilities already exist.

### The Potential of VoIP

■ The voice portal market will reach $5 billion by 2005. (The Kelsey Group)

■ Enterprises will migrate their voice from traditional networks to data networks at a rate that will create a $16.5-billion-dollar IP-PBX market worldwide by 2006. (Allied Business Intelligence)

■ The unified messaging market is expected to reach $31 billion by 2006. (Intellicomm Inc.)

■ The wireless instant messaging subscriber base is expected to grow to more than 43 million by 2004. (IDC)

■ More than two billion people will use Internet voice portals, voice-enabled Web sites, and Web-based IVR systems by 2005. (Davidson Consulting)

■ There will be 71 million voice portal users by 2005, up from 4.4 million users in 2001. (Allied Business Intelligence)

■ 90 percent of enterprises with multiple locations will start switching to IP systems for voice in the next five years. (Phillips Group)

VoIP solutions are already meeting, and in some cases exceeding, the quality or "carrier grade" of traditional PSTNs and enabling much richer consumer offerings. By 2007, industry analysts believe that VoIP will account for almost 75 percent of the world's voice services. A new age in communications is upon us.

## Enabling Convergence

Today, I am involved in creating products and participating in research fueled by the increased popularity of IP telephony—the primary technology that enables convergence. In Chapter 2, I discuss our corporate history and the sequence of events that gave birth to the Net2Phone technology, which is used and licensed by a number of industry participants. The quick history is that IDT, a low-cost world carrier and prepaid company, which was founded by Howard Jonas, created Net2Phone. Today Net2Phone develops tools that will be used in whatever IP communications services and applications are developed in the future—it is no longer about cheap phone calls.

There are several ways to measure the potential of convergence through VoIP—by minutes, by capital investment, by revenue per services—and tables and charts with these indicators are spread throughout the book. All of these are important metrics that reflect the expansion of communications convergence.

VoIP's goal is to achieve widespread, richer connectivity through a single device. The personal computer, TV, and telephone have certain capabilities, but VoIP will combine these machines into "unified" function devices. The immediate advantages of VoIP are its ability to deliver low-cost, long-distance phone service and to create a unified network capable of supporting a variety of different platforms. IP packets include text, video, and audio. Because IP networks are high-bandwidth, they make more efficient use of that bandwidth by compressing data and allowing for multiple transmissions over the same line. What's more, IP networks can be combined with intelligent software tools to create smart devices and smart applications designed to provide seamless, natural, and meaningful communication.

As the COO of Net2Phone, I traveled quite a bit to discuss the VoIP opportunity with network, cable, and telecommunications providers. What I learned was that the number one concern of the major players is the ability to implement a reliable, large-scale network, to guarantee call delivery from end to end. The technology identifies not only failures and faults but also targets suspicious behavior and can repair problems without direct human intervention. Net2Phone can turn gateways off and on, reload software, reboot them, and do everything remotely except physically pull out hardware pieces.

Net2Phone's advances gave birth to the VoIP network

management tool, Voxis. Early on at Net2Phone, engineers learned that traditional monitoring capabilities are heavy and inadequate for the kind of relationship that management systems need with remote gateways. Simply asking, "Are you still alive?" or being notified of errors (through SNMP) is not sufficient when you have a quality issue. You need to monitor how well you are doing on a constant basis, whether your efforts are being thwarted by the rest of the network, whether there is any indication of problems in the network. There are subjective quality issues that call for a hand-holding or a streaming relationship with the devices, rather than an on-demand polling relationship. It's like having a teacher watch students in a class on a constant basis, rather than asking each one individually whether he or she is all right.

In addition, we learned that although the gateway gave us a fair amount of information about what was happening to it, we could see failures in the PSTN interfaces to the network. It is not uncommon for those lines to be down, to get misdirected, or to get a fast busy because of overload. We needed to be able to verify even those PSTN connections that were outside the traditional VoIP area. For this we need we created "dialers" that constantly dial into the gateways through the PSTN interface.

Besides querying the gateways on their status, we also needed to monitor the transport capability of the network itself by sending test packets and seeing how they were doing. We therefore created what we called a world of "streamers." Streamers are devices that stream voice packets to each other on a constant basis and monitor them. The streamer results are passed back to Voxis for a single view of the network.

So, Voxis is not only watching gateways; it is also getting input from dialers that are trying to dial into the system and from streamers that are distributed at points of presence throughout the network and are trying to send voice packets around the network. Voxis also gets input from the most valuable input source, which we called the "miners." Miners are software that basically "mine" the very recent history of everything that's going on in the network. There's a lot of information inherent in the network that can be derived only by comparing recent trend data from multiple places or multiple gateways. It's a level of artificial intelligence not dissimilar to mining data to ferret out long-term trends.

---

**VoIP is the first real-time application in IP.**

---

All of these solutions, combined, feed into the Voxis dashboard. We also envisioned a self-healing capability. To "self heal," Voxis passes directions to the actual routing tables of the network, ensuring in real time that traffic is successfully routed where it should be. Voxis will ultimately offer service providers a level of quality and reliability that exceeds those of traditional circuit-switched networks.

VoIP is the first synchronous or real-time application on IP. The "data" Web itself is asynchronous. That means that if packets of data don't get where they're supposed to, they are automatically re-sent. That's not real-time communications. Voice puts the demand of real-time synchronicity on the network, and therefore the network needs Voxis. We see the large service providers, Tier 1 providers, large top carriers worldwide, and thousands of broadband providers worldwide as customers for the Voxis product.

## Where It Will Take Us

Internet telephony has advanced significantly in the past several years. As we've just discussed, QoS has improved, stability of applications has increased, and reliability of the total user experience is greater. In fact, the robust nature of the marketplace feeds into what Net2Phone has been saying all along—that the success of the market is dependent on the ability to deliver reliable commercial grade service. Through Voxis, this is now a reality.

The services we discuss today in conjunction with VoIP are voice portals, advanced messaging, IP audio- and video-conferencing, and ecommerce solutions. The real challenge is to expand on this thinking and to apply the functionality that exists in these services to devices and services other than PCs and telephones. This is where wireless and cable technologies come into play. The services that will succeed are likely those that are created without the mindset of the traditional "wired" telephony world. We need to rethink and re-examine the industry without the bias and limitations of the past hundred years of telephony history. If you don't disconnect yourself from the Old World, you tend to simply rework the old stuff. And the real value-added applications—the real win here—will come out of left field and will not be tied to the way that people communicate today.

---

Dramatic technology development requires that you start from scratch with an empty whiteboard.

---

There is probably a better way for us to communicate than via the standard telephone, for a number of reasons. Communicating in a group of two is a limited form—in our lives, we do not normally communicate one-on-one. Communication, after all, comes from the word "community"; communities often consist of more than two people. We need to introduce the idea of talking in a community structure in a more free-form, open way than the one-to-one interaction that takes place over the telephone.

As services become more distributed and content richer, more unlike the traditional telephone call, we'll begin to see an impact among customers. Community-enabled services that users can easily enable or disable, the ability to quickly link multiple legs of calls, and the capacity to include video in their communications are examples of these services. Customers will also see the integration of wireless, PDA, and telephony devices in these processes. These new types of services cannot be easily accomplished, if they can be accomplished at all, in the traditional PSTN world; this will be the real demarcation that will fuel customer acceptance.

The cable opportunity for convergence is incredible. Cable homes will be using the same connections not only for delivering "TV"-like images but also for the converged communications stream, "interactive TV."

## Word on the Street

Although Wall Street has been down on high-tech, it is still true that if Wall Street analysts and investors sniff out an opportunity that has value, they will come. The simple truth is that telecommunications is what makes the world work—literally. Analysts, investors, and managers need to perceive the value that convergent services will bring not only to the telecommunications and Internet industries but also to media, entertainment, and financial services.

The financial industry is one of the primary users of VoIP solutions. Rob McCormick, CEO of Savvis Communications, works with firms such as Merrill Lynch, offering it network solutions for the millions of transactions that take place in its branch offices all over the world. The complexity of the data being processed, the need for a seamless and reliable network, and the opportunity to add a human element to the mix has drastically updated financial services. Savvis specializes in virtual private networks, but McCormick sees an opportunity for convergent services such as collaborative video that make click-and-trade scenarios practically Neanderthal.

---

"Wall Street funded a lot of network companies that did not have good business plans, but this doesn't change the fact that network technology is the PC technology of this decade."

—Rob McCormick, Chairman and CEO, Savvis Communications

---

## Adding Greater Value for Investors

One of the ways that Adir and its parent company is adding value for investors is through acquisitions and partnerships. Adir's acquisition of NetSpeak, for example, reinforced commitment among its shareholders and significantly expanded the company's customer base. NetSpeak was identified as a company that could add to Adir's suite of products and help it further penetrate new customer bases. It also created numerous industry partnerships to position itself better.

---

### Potential for IP Telephony and Voice Services

- Worldwide IP telephony revenue will grow from $500 million in 1999 to $18.7 billion in 2004 (106 percent growth). (IDC)
- Enhanced services revenue will increase from $270 million in 1999 to $12.6 billion in 2004. (Ovum)
- By the year 2002, nearly 30 percent of international phone traffic will be carried over data lines, up from only 0.2 percent in 2001. (Probe)
- Industry analysts estimate that VoIP services revenue will grow to approximately $23 billion in 2004. (Kagoor)

---

NetSpeak had developed the end-to-end delivery process for marketing, sales, installation, and support of VoIP solutions worldwide. In addition, its solutions were more mature, more thoroughly tested, and successfully installed around the world. Adir saw the NetSpeak opportunity as giving it a quick entry and new products for many of the next-generation telcos that are looking for solutions. As technology matures, there is often consolidation among players, particularly those who have pieces of solutions. We expect that there will be consolidation in the VoIP industry; Adir's acquisition of NetSpeak supports that trend.

Throughout this book, I examine the types of services, products, relationships, and activities specific companies are undertaking to further develop the IP telephony space. Spread throughout these chapters are also mini-case studies of the most prominent companies in telecommunications in both the services and the technology sectors.

## Notes

1. Davidson Consulting, CommWebb, www.commweb.com.
2. The International Engineering Consortium, Syndeo Corporation, "The Coming of True Convergence: Why Service Providers Can Finally Turn Out the Lights on the Old Public Switched Telephone Network," www .iec.org.
3. National Convergence Alliance, Inc. "The State of Convergence: Its Role Today and for the Future," 2000, www.convergencealliance.com.

# Two Hot Dogs with Mustard:
## Our Humble Beginnings

IDT Telecom and Net2Phone are a family of fairly sophisticated technology companies that are leading advances in the telecommunications industry. However, its beginnings were decidedly low-tech—in fact, you could say that it all began with hot dogs.

In his book *On a Roll: From Hot Dog Buns to High Tech Millions* (Viking, 1998), Howard Jonas, who founded IDT, tells the story of his entrepreneurial awakenings at the age of fourteen, when he opted for self-employment and bought a hot dog stand rather than work at a demanding butcher shop. Howard is a great storyteller, and I've been lucky to hear the IDT history firsthand.

Today, IDT provides much of the infrastructure and retail relationships for communications. Howard Jonas founded IDT in the late 1980s as a newsletter publishing company. At that time, Marc Knoller was his head of sales. Marc proved to be an invaluable employee—dedicated and results oriented—and the little company took off. Marc soon was considered Howard's righthand man at IDT. So when he announced that he was resigning in order to move to Israel with his family, Howard was understandably distraught. Howard's solution was to make IDT a global company, with Marc running the sales operation from Israel. In theory, this was a great idea, and when Marc became situated in Israel, he kept up the pace of sales he had established prior to the move. The problem? Incredibly large phone bills! Pragmatic, yet undaunted, Howard and Marc devised a "callback" system where international calls were conducted over U.S. phone lines, thereby dispensing with the international call fee. This worked so well that Howard, while on vacation in Israel himself, proclaimed that telecom was to be the new focus of his company. In fact, IDT was going to make a business out of the callback technology that he and Marc had created.

Up until this point, there was no such thing as a callback system. It was technologically a tremendous advancement in communications, but as to whether it would run into regulatory problems—no one was sure. This is why, when IDT launched its first product, in 1990, the company was cited as igniting a communications revolution. Luckily for Howard and IDT, there were no regulations barring his system, which provided international calling service at inexpensive rates and over U.S. lines (although that's not how AT&T saw it—but more on that in a moment).

Soon, IDT was a facilities-based, multinational carrier routing more than eight billion minutes of traffic annually. Today, IDT Telecom, managed by Motti Lichtenstein, uses its own telecommunications backbone and fiber optic network infrastructure to provide services to its carrier customers. It's a carrier's carrier. It also has a prepaid telecom business with more than $1 billion in revenue. Over the years, many talented communications professionals, including Howard Balter, Geoff Rochwarger, Moshe Kagnoff, Jonathan Levy, and Joshua Winkler, have helped to fuel IDT's success. Headquartered in Newark, New Jersey, IDT made its entry into the world of telecommunications via a wild ride that was characteristic of Howard's approach to business and reflective of his entrepreneurial personality.

Even in the early days of the Internet, telecommunications was a highly competitive, eat-or-be-eaten type of business. Two events that have now become legend are Howard's development of the callback technology despite opposition from AT&T and his success in convincing the cable pioneer John Malone to invest in IDT.

## David vs. Goliath: IDT Takes on AT&T

Like that between Superman and Lex Luthor, the relationship between Howard and AT&T was complicated. He admired its dominance of the marketplace but also felt that IDT was a worthy competitor with both advanced technology and the wherewithal to move quickly and accept risk and as such represented the future of telecom. In his book, *On a Roll*, Howard tells the story of how his then-small company won an historic victory against AT&T. He describes it as a David-versus-Goliath story that played out in the halls of the White House when AT&T challenged the very nature of IDT's callback system. IDT's callback system was designed to offer international customers an inexpensive alternative to making calls over the large telco's international lines by allowing callers to reroute international calls through U.S. exchanges, bypassing non-U.S. carriers' higher rates. By using the callback system, the person initiating the call does not incur an international call fee. AT&T claimed that for every call that went unanswered over its international lines to trigger the callback process, costs were indeed incurred with the callback system and that these costs were going unpaid. In effect, it said, this was theft of service; IDT was stealing from AT&T.

In reality, it seemed that this was strategic maneuvering on the part of AT&T, whose very policies ensured that no costs were charged for incomplete calls. But the damage had been done and the Federal Communications Commission (FCC) notified. It was due to make a decision on this usage within a few weeks. If the ruling went against IDT, the small carrier would not survive. To make matters worse, Howard couldn't get through to anyone at the FCC, nor would any reporters cover the story until after the ruling had been made. Until, that is, a lone reporter from Forbes did a piece about the nuances of the case that was published two weeks before the ruling was scheduled to be made. Inexplicably, the ruling was delayed—long enough for Howard to use one of his Washington, D.C., contacts to win him an audience with then Vice President Dan Quayle. Vice President Quayle and Dan McIntosh, the head of the Competitiveness Council at the time, met with Howard to discuss the FCC's concerns and committed to reviewing all of the facts in the case; if IDT's position panned out, Howard had the support of the White House. And the rest is history—today, IDT is a multi-billion-dollar company. Always the competitor, Howard celebrated the victory with a new sales campaign. To the delight of his supporters and employees, from then on potential IDT customers were invited to call 1-800-SCREW-ATT.

| IDT Timeline | |
| --- | --- |
| 1990 | Founded by Howard Jonas. |
| 1996 | Introduced carrier service. |
| March 1996 | IDT went public. |
| July 1996 | Launched Net2Phone. |
| July 1996 | Released the VoIP technology that would cut the cost of international calls by 95 cents. To |

| | launch it, Sara Grosvenor, a great-grand-daughter of Alexander Graham Bell, used the technology to place the company's first phone call from New York over the network to Susan Cheever, a great-granddaughter of Thomas Watson, in London. |
|---|---|
| July 1997 | Entered prepaid calling market. |
| February 1998 | IDT filed for secondary offering of common stock. |
| July 1999 | Net2Phone IPO. |
| December 1999 | Net2Phone filed for secondary offering of common stock. |
| August 2000 | IDT brokered the partnership between Net2-Phone and AT&T. |

## "The Malone Memo"

Outside Howard's office at IDT hangs a framed, four-page note handwritten on yellow legal paper and addressed to the Liberty Media founder and chairman John Malone. John is a communications visionary who assembled TCI, a large cable empire, and sold it to AT&T for $140 billion, becoming the largest shareholder in AT&T and a board member. The letter is a draft of the thank-you note Howard sent John after their first meeting, at which Howard convinced the media mogul to invest in IDT. And invest he did. John, then an AT&T director, persuaded AT&T to invest in IDT. In his letter to John, Howard called their five-hour meeting in Denver the greatest opportunity he'd ever had in his life and said he'd left the meeting with the conviction that IDT was a perfect partner for John's forceful Liberty Media. Howard commented on the similarities between the two men. Howard and John were able to open up, despite the fact that John has been characterized by some writers, including Ken Auletta, as an extremely private person, who in his "business life, strives for pure logic unalloyed by emotion, unswayed by friendship or sentiment. He is a man of science."[1]

In my view, both men are visionaries and incredibly gifted thinkers. John is a mathematician from Yale, while Howard hails from Harvard. Though John has often been thought of as aloof, Howard has been described by some reporters in a more personal tone as having the "wit and verve of a standup comic."[2]

But Howard had a point. As I've worked with him over the years, it's clear that he and John share the same values, work ethic, creativity, and goal orientation, and this has made their partnership work. These are characteristics that are shared by the entire IDT/Net2Phone team. As a result of their meeting, Liberty Media took a 10 percent stake in IDT, and John worked with Howard to secure a $1.4 billion investment by AT&T in Net2Phone. In addition to investors like AT&T and Liberty Media, IDT has used acquisitions to expand its market reach and developed exclusive relationships with a host of worldwide service providers. (See Table 2-1.)

## The Cowboy and the Businessman

John Malone's history in telecom is fascinating, and correlates well with Howard's own career. Both admired AT&T, both sought it out as a partner, and I consider both to be visionaries in their own right. Recognizing that cable can bridge the "last mile," AT&T bought Malone's TCI in 1998 for an unprecedented $52 billion. After the AT&T divesture, each Regional Bell Operating Company (RBOC) was given a geographical region and a "last mile" connection directly to the home. AT&T became primarily a long distance carrier. As the divestiture proceeded, the RBOCs were beginning to compete in the long-distance market, threatening AT&T's long-distance business. And while AT&T had other business

**Table 2-1. IDT acquisition history.**

| Acquisition | Date Announced | Date Completed | Purchase Price ($ Millions) | Business |
|---|---|---|---|---|
| **Assets of PCIX** | N/A | August 1996 | $1.5 | Alliance partner |
| **Internat Computer Systems** | N/A | October 1996 | $3.0 | Alliance partner |
| **Rock Enterprises** | 9/11/97 | November 1997 | $5.3 | Consultant to IDT |
| **50% of UTA** | 3/24/98 | May 1998 | $2.65 | Debit card distributor |
| **Interexchange** | 4/23/98 | May 1998 | $129.2 | Debit card service platform |
| **Orion Telekom BV** | 2/23/99 | | Not disclosed | European long distance carrier |
| **ZAO Investelectrosvyaz of Moscow, Russia** | N/A | November 2000 | $9 | Telecom |
| **PT-1 Debit Card Business** | 1/29/01 | February 2001 | Not disclosed | Debit card |

interests, the long-distance market provided one of its significant revenue streams.

The specific threat was losing the U.S market, where AT& T couldn't deliver a call without paying dues to a RBOC. AT& T's solution was to buy TCI and grab the opportunity to compete with the RBOCs by owning the "last mile" to the home. Malone understood that this purchase was premised on moving AT&T's core network to Voice Over IP. Clearly Net2-Phone's technology could take John's cable networks and turn them into voice-carrying networks.

Net2Phone continues to receive support from its parent, IDT, and from its key investor, John Malone. Both IDT and John believe in the goals of Net2Phone and are committed to its success. This helped in October 2001 when AT&T sold most of its stake in Net2Phone to IDT and Liberty Media. IDT, Liberty, and AT&T together formed an ownership consortium that totals 49 percent of the company's equity and 60 percent of its voting rights.

## From Callback to Full-Scale Carrier: The Birth of Net2Phone

Within IDT and with John Malone as an investor, Howard assembled an enviable team to help develop IDT into a full-scale carrier. Jonas and his team transformed IDT from a callback company into a carrier's carrier and took it into the prepaid calling market. I joined Net2Phone and immersed myself immediately in the opportunity.

Originally, Net2Phone had operated within IDT, and it was not until 1997 that it became a subsidiary. Net2Phone's core business strategy was, and still is, to market its services worldwide and through marquee partners such as AOL, Yahoo!, and IBM. To provide these next-generation services, advanced technology was needed, and this is where Net2-

Phone's true value proposition emerged. Under the direction of Howie Balter as CEO, the Net2Phone technology resulted in a number of exclusive, lucrative deals that ultimately won the company two-thirds of the retail Internet telephony market.

Howard had emphasized the greater role cable will have for companies like IDT and Net2Phone. IDT and Net2Phone emerged with advanced technology just as the Internet itself was starting to take shape, and have provided leading technology in this area ever since. The aim was to do the same for cable telephony.

Net2Phone is a leading service provider for Web-enabled telephony and has received numerous industry awards; it has also been acknowledged as a leader in Internet telephony by the analysts at major investment houses. Its services allow calls to be made from PC to phone, as well as from phone to phone, over IP lines. It is the advanced VoIP technology that was created at Net2Phone that makes these services possible.

## The IPO

One of the most exhilarating experiences I have had in my career was being a part of the team that took Net2Phone public and then watching as its performance level and customer base skyrocketed. Net2Phone had Cliff Sobel as chairman (he is now the U.S. ambassador to the Netherlands), Howie Balter as CEO, Ilan Slasky as CFO, and Jeff Goldberg as CTO. We had a hugely successful IPO and assembled a world-class team of professionals. When we were preparing for the IPO, everything was done off-hours and under a lot of pressure. We had to get things done immediately and with whatever resources we had available. There is always an adrenaline rush in fast-paced business maneuverings, but the frenzied state caused by the IPO made things even more exciting.

Net2Phone's IPO days were heady ones. Mordy Rothberg was Net2Phone's executive vice president of sales. We were working diligently to solicit large phone carriers and Internet companies to become Net2Phone customers and partners, including investment giants. Mordy is wonderful relationship builder, and we used to joke that Mordy literally knew everyone everywhere. In fact, he so charmed Masayoshi Son, the head of Softbank, that the company became a Net2-Phone partner

---

**The only thing that is really sustainable is a good business model.**

---

Out of everyone on the team at that time, the one individual who truly stood out was Howie Balter, who subsequently left Net2Phone in October 2001. At the time of the IPO, Howie was clearly a star. He had an unbelievable ability to crystallize and simplify business objectives, opportunities, and models. It always appeared that no matter how astute and sophisticated the bankers were, Howie was able to outshine them all. He had the unique ability to dissect a financial model and stick it back together in a way that made it infinitely clearer. Howie and his CFO, Ilan Slasky, were incredible assets for us, particularly in those early IPO days when there was so much hype around technology companies that it was hard to know what was an opportunity and what wasn't. Howie always had the ability to identify an opportunity and to articulate his thinking calmly and clearly. When the rest of the world was putting out press releases for every little thing, Net2Phone was building a business.

### Net2Phone Highlights

| | |
|---|---|
| 1995 | Announced plans to release first PC-to-phone technology. |
| July 1996 | Net2Phone 4.62 beta PC Client half-duplex launched November. |
| October 1996 | Announced plans to release Net2Phone Direct. |
| September 1997 | Net2Phone Direct (phone-to-phone over IP) launched in the United States. |
| May 1999 | Net2Phone filed for initial public offering. |
| July 1999 | Net2Phone completed initial public offering of common stock. |
| November 1999 | Net2Phone filed for secondary offering of common stock; Net2Phone v.10, the all-in-one communications software, unveiled. |
| January 2000 | Net2Phone rolled out international phone-to-phone IP voice service. |
| August 2000 | AT&T invested $1.4 billion in Net2Phone (32% economic stake). |
| June 2001 | Net2Phone introduced Broadband Voice Solutions. Liberty Media and Net2Phone entered multi-year technology licensing agreement. France Telecom interconnected with Net2Phone's Voice Over IP network for carrier-grade interconnection. |
| August 2001 | Net2Phone launched CommCenter PC calling software. |
| October 2001 | Net2Phone announced new investor, ownership structure. Net2Phone provided Microsoft Windows XP Users with expanded network capabilities. |
| June 2002 | Net2Phone launched first outsourced Voice Solution for cable operators. |

For the team, there was an excitement throughout the whole Net2Phone process because it was impossible *not* to see that this type of technology was going to change the whole spectrum of communications. It was clear that the Internet was on its way to becoming more than a telephone network or standalone TV system ever could. Future possibilities were being presented that, at the time, we couldn't even imagine becoming realities. But we sensed it. We knew this technology was going to ignite serious, cross-industry change. A worldwide superhighway was now going to carry voice, and Net2Phone would be a leader in unfolding that exciting technology. To participate in bringing this technology to the world has been deeply satisfying.

The partners solicited as initial investors in Net2Phone were AOL, GE Capital, and Softbank. Everyone we spoke to shared our clear belief that this technology was going to create a sea change in communications. The company went IPO and adopted the ticker NTOP in July 1999.

The press was also reinvigorated by what Net2Phone was doing. The news resuscitated the telephone and telecommunications industry. The company's leaders found themselves on the covers of magazines that normally featured technology pioneers such as Bill Gates, Michael Dell, and Andy Grove.

The Net2Phone technology has outlived the dot.com frenzy and will take its place in the annals of industry history as one of those advances that made a dramatic difference and had a major impact on the world we live in.

## The Birth of Adir

As a major spokesman for Net2Phone, I spent a great deal of time trying to spread the message about this opportunity. It was exciting to sell the vision of convergence, what to me was a convergence of server-based intelligence, a uniform worldwide network, and the capability of transmitting voice and video over that one network. I traveled the world often with Mordy Rothberg to promote the idea of convergence and the Net2Phone technology to large carriers in order to forge relationships. Every time my hosts learned about the network management capability that was possible, the response was phenomenal. This was confirmation that the network management technology that we had created at Net2Phone would be very valuable for large carriers around the world.

## The Partners and Their Approach

Network management was about monitoring the hardware gateways around the network. Net2Phone received expressions of interest from several such gateway manufacturers but took its time deciding which one to pursue. The first interest came from one of the largest telephone switch manufacturers in the world. The relationship made sense to both parties, and negotiations began.

We had several high-level meetings, culminating in a draft letter of intent from the manufacturer committing to sell the Adir solution with its gateways. But, after consideration, we felt that the terms being offered were not significant enough. Yet, this experience confirmed that Net2Phone's technology was two years ahead of anything else that was being developed.

The next opportunity came from a large switch manufacturer based in Europe. Mordy Rothberg and I flew to Europe several times for meetings. Ultimately, the company committed to giving us $500,000 to test our VoIP solutions. The relationship was a positive one, except that it was just not moving as fast as we would have liked. We were somewhat concerned that this company's adoption of our technology would not proceed as rapidly as needed to compete in a very volatile marketplace.

### "The Cisco Solution"

We had previously discussed our technology with Cisco. During one Cisco sales call to Net2Phone, we arranged a conference call between the Cisco technical people and Net2Phone. We arranged for a meeting in New Jersey between the Cisco VoIP team and our own staff. About eight Cisco representatives visited us in our labs in Lakewood to dissect and discuss the technology we had built. Cisco wanted to move into the carrier market, and the Net2Phone technology was designed to provide the redundancy and scalability that large carriers needed. Allistair Woodman, the director of Cisco's VoIP initiative, saw the value in our technology and envisioned how it would help Cisco's customers. This marked the beginning of a very harmonious relationship and was an auspicious beginning for Adir. Cisco data routers managed 70 percent of the data in the world, and it was now our network management solutions that would help Cisco succeed in the voice space. The partnership with Cisco set in motion the Adir spinoff.

There were several reasons for creating Adir. As a rule, businesses do not invest money in a company that is a customer—it sets a bad precedent to invest in one customer over another. Thus, Cisco could not invest directly in Net2Phone. Additionally, the technology would be purchased more readily by other service providers if it did not come from Net2Phone itself, because companies do not want to buy solutions from their competitors. Once it was clear that Cisco was investing, investments came from companies other than those with which we had ongoing relationships, such as Softbank Venture Capital and IDT.

## Adir's Goal

Adir's initial goal was to provide the core solution for enabling VoIP on behalf of the large telco carriers and cable companies worldwide. The customers we are dealing with need systems that are failproof and that can be provisioned easily, tolerate error and accidental user error, and stand up to challenges all around them. To execute that vision, we have to provide software with "five nines" of reliability. Our relationship with IDT was also beneficial. IDT provides guidance and offers contacts and relationships that we continue to leverage. At any point in time, we can use these relationships in operations, logistics, finance, technology, and sales.

In the next few chapters, I present the potential for convergence from the market's perspective and the role of the telecommunications industry in supporting convergence and VoIP.

## Notes

1. Ken Auletta, *The Highwaymen* (New York: Random House, 1997), p. 27.
2. Knight-Ridder Business News, "Newark, NJ-Based Telecommunications Firm's Boss Builds an Empire," May 14, 2001.

# CHAPTER THREE

# Selling the Dream

Successfully introducing a new service or technology into the commercial marketplace involves the efforts of a broad team of professionals. The company's shareholders, financiers, investors, partners, and employees all have a role in identifying and executing the company's vision. As a champion for convergence, I have always concentrated on selling the *vision* of convergence, rather than focusing solely on the underlying technology.

My colleagues and I have consistently sent the message that convergence represents a melding of intelligence; it constitutes a worldwide-unified network that transmits voice and video simultaneously. This vision of intelligence throughout the network and of a technology that intersperses voice with data was an exciting, albeit complicated, one to execute. But those of us who became advocates of IP telephony were firmly committed to the realization that it was just this type of convergent communications that was missing from mainstream telco networks and services. To translate this realization into a vision and then create an executable strategy for bringing that vision to life took an extraordinary team effort that was supported by strong leaders, a sound business model, and a risk-averse organizational culture. This chapter in part chronicles the IDT family's pursuit of its vision of convergence and the strategies that brought this dream to life.

## Vision and Leadership

Howard Jonas, the founder of IDT, was among the first to articulate the vision of IP telephony, where all traffic flowed over an IP infrastructure and VoIP was the natural solution to managing the network. The complex requirements of running voice and video over one homogeneous network include everything from verifying the quality of the transmission and accessing calling routes to devising a pricing scheme for far-ranging types of service. Another issue is educating the market as convergent services continue to evolve into more sophisticated offerings involving a greater number of applications and the devices over which they can be delivered.

As a company pioneering IP telephony and convergence with VoIP, Net2Phone focused both on developing a technology that was scalable and changing its own image from that of a PC-to-phone telco company to that of a company that could send transmissions through all types of devices. To accomplish this, the Net2Phone team needed to be a tightly knit unit that shared the same vision and goals and encompassed the same work ethic. Net2Phone has come to have the largest deployment of VoIP solutions, and its technology, now developed and licensed by Adir, leads the competition. This was possible because early on we made an effort to try different things, and the entrepreneurial spirit that came naturally to us further fueled this endeavor.

As the Net2Phone team came together, it was clear that the group mirrored the sentiments of the entire company. Net2Phone was formally organized to nurture a spirit of collaboration, risk taking, speed, and flexibility. It is interesting to me that these business strategies have been analyzed and written about for the past ten years by management theorists like Gary Hamel and C. K. Prahalad, in their classic work *Competing for the Future,* and by Jon Katzenbach, in *The Wisdom of Teams*; in our case, we were doing it almost intuitively.

The teams I participated in were as singleminded in their focus on developing a world-class suite of products and services as they were in perpetuating the convergence phenomenon. And we did this in an all-out way. Other companies were spending an inordinate amount of time on testing varying levels of IP telephony in select markets. But these trials focused more on arbitrage or pricing issues than on the actual service, which we believed should promote the idea of convergence. We felt that if interest in IP telephony focused on pricing, the industry and marketplace weren't going to view it as a potential killer application. Our perspective was to keep adding services that would change consumer behavior; and in this way, IP telephony with VoIP would reach killer app status.

## Adir's Vision

Adir was conceived with the vision to provide large carriers and cable companies with the solutions needed to enable IP telephony worldwide. This vision required a company that truly understood its customers' needs for failproof systems that could be easily provisioned, that tolerated errors, and that could stand up to the challenges of an evolving marketplace. The solutions used by Net2Phone and further developed by Adir addressed each of these needs. That we had reached this understanding can be credited to our original design team, headed by Jeff Goldberg. Jeff was the leader of the team that developed Net2Phone's VoIP technology. Many on his team were trained at Bell Labs. Their background ensured a deep awareness of how the large carriers were approaching opportunities in IP telephony and the challenges and barriers they faced in rolling out convergent services.

When Net2Phone first introduced its VoIP solution, the company was two years ahead of what others in the industry were doing. Net2Phone and now Adir remain technologically competitive by remaining constantly vigilant as to what their competitors are doing, analyzing new technologies, and gathering customer feedback that enables the companies to assess customer needs. They also constantly reexamine their own work in identifying opportunities for developing new solutions or creating new markets.

Once it established a deep knowledge of its customers' needs and understood how those needs might change, Adir set about expanding its scope of operations and influence. To do this, it needed to be sure that its vision was communicated well within the company and that its culture supported the company's vision, strategic objectives, and operations.

## Communicating the Vision

The Adir team was able to execute its vision of creating the solutions that would allow for convergence by being technologically ahead of the game and by fostering a close-knit, familial culture. Adir modeled itself after its parent and grandparent companies—this came easily, since, in its earliest days, Adir was made up of a core group of people from Net2Phone. The vision was communicated easily because almost everyone at Adir had been involved in its creation and had worked on the plan to bring it to fruition.

## Everyone Is a Participant

As Adir grew and we began to recruit from external sources, we were deliberate in interviewing and hiring people who understood and were in sync with the company's vision and goals. This was reinforced in weekly meetings and further supported by a companywide team structure. We viewed our organization as being a unified team, and the nature of teamwork guarantees that information gets communicated. When managers consider employees and colleagues as equals who share the same goals, and not as minions, the successful communication and execution of those goals are practically guaranteed. Or, at least, this was my experience.

---

The nature of teamwork guarantees that things get communicated.

---

We found that there is less chance of making an error in understanding goals when they are created and constructed in a group arena. When everyone is a participant, each individual can hear all of the concerns and issues. This thinking extends to external relationships, as well. When we seek out partners or companies for acquisition, we look for companies that have an approach similar to ours. (Netspeak, for instance, possessed the products and customer base that would make Adir an even stronger player, but what proved to be most attractive about the company was that it had a vision similar to ours and operated in teams.)

This type of organizational culture and operational cohesiveness doesn't come easily. We spent a great amount of time early on mapping out what we wanted the company to become and addressing the immediate operational and organizational challenges.

## Organization and Culture: "The Human Side of the Enterprise"

### Find the Right Place for the Right Person
A handful of attributes that characterize the Adir organization fall, in the popular business lexicon, under the rubric of

value-based management thinking. First, at Adir we believe in being open to ideas from all of our employees. I believe it is important that each individual be comfortable in being heard and that each person know that he or she will always be heard. It has been my experience that people inherently want to do the right thing; this leads to the belief that you will never go wrong if you trust your people.

Douglas McGregor, one of the forefathers of management theory and a seminal business thinker, debunked Taylorism with a similar view. McGregor was a management theorist at MIT in the early 1960s, a time when humanistic thinking with regard to the workplace was practically nonexistent. Yet, today, McGregor's views of employees as self-motivated and trustworthy decision makers—what he called the human side of the enterprise—have influenced modern business thinking.

We, too, believe that people naturally want to do the right thing. Toward this end, we invest in them, give them guidance, teach them, and help them to do their jobs better. In their role as leaders, managers need to realize that there is a place for everyone in an organization and that it is the manager's job to figure out what that place is and put the person there. It's not about removing a "problem" through firing, disciplinary action, or a lateral move. As a leader, you need to find the right place for each employee—and if the employee's needs and skills change, then you need to put that person in a better place. But the right thing to do is to work with that individual to find a position that plays to his or her skills and strengths.

---

Find the right place for each employee.

---

### Function as a Team

The second aspect of Adir's culture that has strengthened the organization is that we are literally bereft of traditional politicking. Early in the company's life, each employee success depended on individual merit and the ability to work as part of a team. This is still true today. Titles have always been secondary. We felt that the company functioned as a team and that titles, title charts, and the like only created dissonance. The company's early leaders, in particular Howard Jonas and Howie Balter, created this mind-set, and it has endured.

### Exercise Moderation

Through a policy of moderate spending, we have remained fiscally sound, which has given the company the ability to sustain an entrepreneurial, risk-taking environment. Even at the market's height, when money flowed into technology and telecommunications companies, we kept our spending habits in check. We did this partly because it was the sensible thing to do, but it also had to do with respect. We respected our investors as partners and as teammates, and we viewed their investment as being precious—it was a sign of their trust in our company. For instance, we didn't and still don't see investing in Super Bowl ads as a smart strategy. Instead, putting our money where it will do the most good, such as in securing important licenses and relationships, is a deliberate choice.

The workspace at IDT, Net2Phone, and Adir reflect this attitude, as well. Along with a lack of titles and to reinforce the team structure, most of us share office space. In fact, Howard Jonas shares an open office with his colleagues. Using space in this way creates an open environment. But there's more to it than that. As individuals and organizations, we never wanted to focus on externalities. Our executive teams don't lead extravagant lifestyles or drive the trendiest cars. And, in truth, in order to preserve the organizational culture of all three companies, we avoid hiring those who do appear arrogant and self-important. These are attributes that would destroy the open, unassuming culture so important to our success.

> ### Traits That Bring Vision to Life
>
> Teamwork: Create an open, collaborative environment.
>
> Values: Apply principles of values-based management.
>
> Moderation: Be financially sensible; treat investments as precious.
>
> Humility: Prize ethics and humility above all else.
>
> Find the whale: Encourage risk taking and the willingness to do the big deal.

## Show Humility

There is a feeling that individual success and those of our companies are a result of divine influence, rather than personal ability. There's no denying that the collaborative efforts of each individual in our company has resulted in a high degree of success; however, that being said, no one assumes an air of self-importance. We have an underlying belief that whatever success we achieve was, in part, ordained. This view is humbling and also nurtures a culture of teamwork and collaboration.

IDT, Net2Phone, and Adir have all been managed with a spirit of generosity, compassion, and kindness. We hold ethics and compassion as two of our strongest and most important attributes, and we treat employees as family. I recall one employee whose family had just lost a member. In a matter of a few hours, Howard Jonas and Howie Balter sought to raise a large sum to help the family in its time of need.

---

Modesty, moderateness, and compassion are three critical attributes for any organization.

---

For this reason, the most difficult time for me personally comes when there is an economic downturn. Laying off people is heart wrenching and particularly difficult for all of us.

## Find the Whale

Because our companies maintain a humanistic approach to business doesn't mean that we aren't fierce competitors. Our teams take pride in being on the forefront of VoIP technology and for their success in maneuvering in a world fraught with volatility. I think that, because our employees want to see their teams and companies enjoy the rewards of success, they push even harder to stay on top in a highly competitive industry.

In addition to teamwork, moderation, and openness, our companies stress the importance of being willing to do *the big deal.* The choice is to either find out where the whale is or spend the whole day fishing for sardines. The financial upside of running a business with a view toward moderation is that we have the capital to do the big deal. Certainly, there is a lot of excitement in making acquisitions or finding new partners and investors. The executive teams of IDT, Net2-Phone, and Adir are adept at identifying important opportunities and then making the deals happen.

Net2Phone's agreement with Netscape reflects this type of thinking: not hubris, but, rather, optimism that we are the right company for those investing in or utilizing VoIP solutions. Early in the life of the Web, we made an exclusive commitment with Netscape that resulted in a multimillion-dollar deal.

---

Find the whale or spend the whole day fishing for sardines.

---

It takes a great deal of guts, commitment, and good will to make these deals happen—particularly when all of our competitors are targeting the same whales. We have been successful in bringing opportunities to fruition by nurturing and developing partnerships based on trust and confidence. It all boils down to four factors. The big deal is predicated on:

1. A social relationship

2. The confidence the two companies have in the product

3. Financial stability

4. The right personnel

## Leading a Visionary Company

When I first joined Adir as its COO and one of its six employees, my goal was to make it a well-oiled, efficient, and powerful organization that could create, sell, and support its products. Job one for me was and still is to make the machine run. To do this effectively, I felt it important to ensure that each person was functioning at his or her optimum. In addition to making sure that our company was functioning at the highest level, there were two other critical aspects to my job.

The second key responsibility I faced was maintaining the business approach we had originally constructed, which was determined to bring value to the company's shareholders. I wanted to ensure that this well-oiled machine would ultimately produce the products that would bring profit and gain to those people who had entrusted us with their investments.

Delivering the message of VoIP to the telcos who were

our customers around the world became my third priority. The message was that we wanted to be their partner in developing products and solutions that would help them succeed with their own customers. We needed the telecommunications world to know that we were ready to work with them in bringing their own services to market.

These responsibilities are still priorities for me today. Adir ultimately achieved all three of these goals and has sustained its performance in these areas. One of the primary reasons for this is that the entire company is constantly assessing how it is doing and what can be done to improve performance. We have embraced the concepts of self-assessment and reinvention and understand that both of these activities are a daily event. But managers shouldn't first reevaluate their organization when the market hits a downturn or some industry phenomenon puts a company in peril.

The personality of our company, and that of our parent and grandparent companies, ensures that as individuals and organizations we are humble and self-motivated. These attitudes reinforce the activities of self-improvement and reinvention and support the occasion when improving might mean doing something dramatic. We're a relatively gutsy group, and we encourage our employees and managers to have the wherewithal and willingness to change direction if that makes sense.

To maintain an edge, companies need:

- Guts
- The interest to constantly examine what they're doing and then to do whatever it takes to rework existing processes and goals to do it better
- To maintain an ongoing vigilance and a willingness to reevaluate themselves and to try new things.

## Remaining on the Cusp with Innovation

At the time that Net2Phone created Adir, it was an industry-held belief that the biggest challenge faced by telcos was the management of a large IP network that would deliver high-quality, reliable convergent services. Net2Phone's VoIP technology, which became Adir's first offering, was the poster product for doing just that. This product remains a major part of the Adir family of solutions.

Our product suite was further strengthened through Adir's acquisition of Netspeak, which contributed several VoIP applications valued by the telcos that already used Adir solutions. These included residential cable, enterprise solutions that allow the user to connect multiple branches of a company over an IP network, and call routing solutions.

One of the biggest impediments to rolling out these services was the confidence level of the telcos. They needed to feel comfortable about what goes on in their networks and what happens with customers. Now bolstered by NetSpeak's products, Adir offers even more unique solutions that deliver this comfort factor. Later in the book, I look at companies that are conducting trials of convergent services in select markets and compare this strategy with those of telcos that are making services immediately available to their customers. My own feeling about trials is that they don't inspire confidence in the service and limit familiarity with the products. Adir prefers to immediately roll out services using its solutions to the consumer and business markets through telcos and cable companies that service these areas.

## Five Will Get You Ten: Deals and Partnerships

Unlike many of its peers in high tech, Adir sought the assistance of partners, rather than venture capitalists and investment bankers, when establishing itself as a separate organization. Because of its link to IDT and Net2Phone, it was able to tap into existing relationships that had been nurtured over time. Softbank, through Gary Rieschel, for example, was a Net2Phone investor and expanded its relationship to become an Adir partner. As a result of its dealings with Softbank and several other companies, Adir never pursued traditional fundraising. However, it was extremely interested in pursuing strategic investors—companies whose names and relationships add more to the company than money—as a means of extending its own reach. It sought out companies with complementary products and services, as well as those that target similar markets. The benefit of this type of strategic relationship was threefold:

1. We believed that an established company that shared our market space would bring additional sales channels.

2. The relationship gave our brand increased credibility.

3. The value and position our company held in the market was further defined and delineated.

It's simple: If you marry a prince, you must be somebody—strategic partnerships brought *relationship value*.

---

**If you marry a prince, you must be somebody.**

---

In identifying and selecting companies with which to partner, we established four criteria. First, we wanted to associate ourselves with companies that were role models for our own company: whom did we want to become? We wanted to become an IBM, and early on companies like IBM became our targets. Second, we also sought out companies whose technology would augment our own. We therefore targeted primarily software companies and equipment manufacturers in telecommunications. Third, we looked for companies that possessed technology that would either augment or extend our own suite of products and services. Fourth, in addition to seeking out investments and strategic relationships to benefit our technology and brand initiatives, we were also interested in expanding the organization through acquisition. This led to Adir's acquisition of NetSpeak, in June 2001.

The investment and strategic partnerships we established were an important way to respond to changes in the industry in terms of business strategies, market demands, and revenue models wrought by the Internet. Software takes time to build. You need to design the product, create a prototype, and then test it with a beta and a golden version. Before the Internet hit the mainstream, companies traditionally followed a somewhat labored process of introducing new products to the marketplace; they planned on having at least one year to roll out a commercial product.. The Internet changed the whole process for creating a new software product. Now, once you announce the introduction of a new product, delivery is expected within a very short time frame. All of the previous phases are condensed into a few stages so that you are practically creating products and delivering them in real time. There is no window to organically build as much as you like. The speed with which dot.com companies evolved and the work ethic needed to establish these companies set a new standard that defined the expectation. All this reset the clock; sixty seconds became one second. These phenomena created new challenges for software companies and made strategic partnering and growth through acquisition two key methods of extending the product line, acquiring new customers, and strengthening brand recognition.

The remaining chapters define and describe IP telephony and convergence in full detail: their market potential, their impact on industry, their most profitable applications, the emerging role of cable broadband in distributing convergent services, and the companies that are spearheading advanced IP technologies and services.

# CHAPTER FOUR

# The New World of Communications:
## The Market's Perspective

Other than the invention of the telegraph, in 1876, nothing else will do so much to revolutionize the way individuals communicate more than IP telephony. The IP network has taken center stage in the global telecommunications industry, driving the convergence of technologies, services, and even industries. Whether your company needs to distribute media-rich content, is looking to reduce the cost of global telephone service, is processing transactions for millions of customers, or is the brains behind a digital TV shopping spree, the IP network is where it all begins, and VoIP technology is the proven solution that adds utility to this unified network.

The IP telephony movement will ultimately force the traditional public switched telephone network (PSTN), which has been the backbone of telecommunications for generations, into obsolescence. Advanced technologies spanning a host of industries are being combined seamlessly and naturally in ways that we have never seen. IP telephony is causing dramatic shifts within the telecommunications industry and among the products and services offered. Because of the flexibility of the IP network and the services enabled by VoIP, businesses are rethinking how they will operate and serve their own customers, technologists are focusing on creating enhanced applications, and consumers are revamping their behavior. That's the exciting part. When people begin to change their behavior, to adopt new attitudes and methods for communicating, then we have crossed into killer app territory. Is VoIP a killer app? Opinions are split on that particular question. I believe that services are being developed right now that are beginning to alter the way people think and act. As these services become more commercialized, VoIP will be embraced by consumers and recognized by the telecom industry as a necessary and critical solution. In actuality, I'm not in favor of describing services as "killer" or "disruptive." If anything, VoIP is the great mediator, taking disparate technologies and applications and unifying them in a fluid and productive way.

In this chapter I share with you what I see as the value and market potential of convergent services and the companies that enable them. In my world, when companies like Cisco, AT&T, and the venture capital community commit heavily to any one technology, it is time to stand up and take notice. If you're the type who pays close attention to the financial and business worlds, then you may have noticed two interconnected themes emerging:

1. The face of communications is evolving radically to focus on IP networks and IP cable as primary infrastructures for sharing information that includes voice, data, and video.

2. CEOs from almost all telecom companies—hardware, software, and carriers alike—are making IP telephony and voice opportunities a core business initiative.

## The Path to Convergence

The ability to transmit voice and data together over an IP network, rather than via a traditional phone line, that delivers the same quality of service (QoS) and applications that we are accustomed to is a milestone in advancing communications convergence. In its current form, the IP network offers a cost-effective medium for long-distance voice and data transmission, as well as for more complex services. An IP network can accommodate a variety of systems, so it creates one seamless network out of many diverse systems. VoIP is a solution—a service, if you will, used by carriers and service providers—that adds functionality to the network, delivering high-quality, simultaneous voice and data transmission. Without VoIP solutions, convergence could not exist. VoIP brings integrity to the IP network and enables more sophisticated functionality. Chapter 5 takes a closer look at the technical details underlying such capabilities.

> VoIP is a service delivered by a variety of carriers and service providers.

The business and consumer markets worldwide have recognized the value of IP telephony. Growth in the international VoIP market has increased dramatically over the past few years, and usage has reached nearly 6.5 billion minutes per year. Another indication of the market's belief that IP telephony is the future of telecommunications is the money that is being invested in the race to develop services and technologies in this sector. More significant, these investments are being made during a time of economic uncertainty. The intense activity in the development, investment, and service arenas reflects the enormous potential of IP telephony. The Cable & Wireless company, for example, has invested more than $2 billion on a global IP network, with the intent of delivering 900 billion minutes by year 2006 (compared to 675 million in 1999).

There is a tremendous amount of activity across the entire tech sector concerning opportunities in IP telephony. In fact, I would have a hard time naming a company that doesn't have some sort of initiative under way. There are the obvious players, like AT&T, Cisco, and 3Com, and the seemingly unlikely Intel and Microsoft. Let's look a little more closely at who the major players are in this arena, the investments, and how the industry is responding to the opportunities presented by IP telephony.

## The Players: Companies to Watch

Companies in the IP telephony space are either technology companies or service providers. Within these categories there exists a great deal of investment activity, whether in the form of licensing deals, alliances, consortiums, partnerships, or acquisitions. The web of relationships that exists among a broad array of organizations involved with IP is quite complex and involves investments from private parties, existing companies, and foreign entities, to name a few. A handful of technology companies dominate the global IP telephony market right now, and most of them are collaborating with each other in some fashion, as part of a partnership, a joint venture, or a licensing arrangement.

3Com, Cisco, Nortel, Lucent, Ericcson, and Alcatel are strong contenders in both the technology and the services arenas. These companies are either developing offerings or working with the major telcos to come up with new consumer and enterprise services. New-generation service providers and product vendors like iBasis, Net2Phone, and MediaRing are developing the solutions that will enable more sophisticated convergent offerings now and in the future as the marketplace matures and customer needs become more complex.

Telecommunications has always been a complex and crowded playing field, but now more than ever companies of all sizes in the most unlikely sectors are getting into the game. We are seeing a great deal of investment activity, not only from Wall Street but also between companies. The hunger for IP telephony services worldwide has created very low barriers to entering the market, and there are about fifty or so minor players managing some very lucrative businesses alongside the big telcos. Throughout 2003 and 2004, a consolidation will occur as markets become more mature and need the support of robust companies that can offer many different types of services.

Market-makers like Cisco recognize that IP telephony and voice services represent the future of telecommunications. They are making strategic moves to drive the evolution of their networking technology, as well as convergent services. In the last year, John Chambers, CEO of Cisco Systems, has made both explicit and implicit comments about the role of IP telephony in his company in terms of projected revenue, the amount of investment dedicated to this effort, and the strategies that are in place to sustain a high level of technological innovation. Ed Paulson, a technology observer of Cisco in particular, believes not only that VoIP is an important part of Cisco's future but that it *is* Cisco's future. Cisco is driving the commercial and enterprise use of IP telephony, adding voice solutions to the networking equipment it offers to its own customers.

The interesting thing about VoIP is that Cisco has integrated these solutions into their products in such a seamless and pervasive way that you don't know you're using it. In Chapter 3, I touched on the reason my company partnered with Cisco and the ways in which our two companies collaborated in bringing IP telephony to the attention of business and industry. A little later in this chapter, I discuss other partnerships worth noting that are driving advances in, and increasing the usage of, IP telephony.

While you would expect vanguard companies like Cisco to move deftly into the IP telephony arena, what's even more fascinating is how many companies outside telecom are getting into the game. Intel has emerged as an 800-pound gorilla, having made a huge investment in its own R&D efforts and taken an active role in developing the standards that govern VoIP. In May 2001, the company released its Intel Converged Communications Platform (ICCP), a hardware and software platform designed to consolidate telephony and business applications from multiple vendors onto a single system. Only a month later, Intel introduced silicon, software, and reference designs for a new Voice Over Packet technology under its Internet Exchange Architecture (IXA). This is the first technology to result from Intel's acquisition of VxTel in February 2001 at a price of $550 million. Intel has been working jointly with Cisco Systems, ITXC, and Lucent Technologies to create a network standard that would allow for interoperability among PCs, personal digital assistants (PDAs), mobile phones, personal gateways, and other digital devices.

## Valuing IP Telephony and Convergence

### Spicing Up the Playing Field

There is and has been over the past twenty-four months a seemingly insatiable desire among high-tech companies to make deals that will provide entrée into the IP telephony market. News of joint ventures, alliances, and acquisitions seems to come every week as industry players look to diversify their portfolios of products and services. A signal event in the industry, and one that reflected the perceived value of IP networking, VoIP, and convergence, was AT&T's investment in Net2Phone. This was widely interpreted by analysts, investors, and industry experts as reflecting AT&T's strong recognition of the technology's potential and indicated a growing confidence in the delivery of converged voice and data.

The purchase, in December 2001, of AT&T's Broadband by Comcast—the third largest cable operator in the United States, with more than 8.4 million subscribers—was a clear statement that included the perceived value of IP telephony in the consumer marketplace. Comcast, and cable operators like it, provide telcos with a way to bridge "the last mile" while providing media-rich content over interactive devices like multimedia PCs or digital televisions. In a joint press release issued by the two companies, AT&T's chairman and CEO, C. Michael Armstrong, said, "AT&T Comcast will create value for its customers, shareowners, and employees by bringing more services to more people more quickly. This is a leap forward in realizing a vision that thousands of AT&T people have worked toward—bringing greater choice in affordable broadband video, voice and data services to even more American homes."[1]

To provide an idea of the pace of acquisitions within the industry that are specifically designed to expand convergence and voice initiatives, see Table 4-1, which presents information on acquisitions in 2000.

Acquisitions and consolidation seemed to reach an all-time high in 2000; however, the pace slowed somewhat in 2001 and 2002. Market penetration reached its threshold for existing services, and the industry itself became saturated by the number of communications companies entering the IP

*(text continues on page 56)*

**Table 4-1. IP telephony acquisitions in 2000.**

| Buyer | Amount ($ Millions) | Company Acquired | Type of Company Acquired |
|---|---|---|---|
| Analog Devices | Not disclosed | Signaling Processing Associates | Supplies voice processing and fax/data software for telecom apps |
| Cisco | 369 (total for Vovida and IPCell) | Vovida | Supplier of networking protocols |
| | | IPCell | Software for broadband access combining IP and telephony service |
| Cisco | 266 | Active Voice | Enterprise messaging |
| Cisco | 175 | Komodo | VoIP devices that allow analog telephones to use IP networks |
| Cisco | 200 | JetCell | Wireless telephony solutions for enterprise networks |
| Dataflex | Not disclosed | Telephony Experts | Billing solutions provider |
| IBasis | 100 | PriceInteractive | Specializes in voice-enabled e-commerce apps |

| ITXC | Not disclosed | OzEmail Interline | VoIP wholesale |
| --- | --- | --- | --- |
| **ITXC** | 151 | Efusion | Software provider of voice web apps |
| **JFAX.com** | 74 | EFax.com | Free fax service provider |
| **Net2Phone** | Not disclosed | Aplio | Makers of standalone VoIP dialers |
| **Net Voice** | Not disclosed | Synetric | Networking company |
| **Pace Micro Technology** | 64 | VegaStream | Specializes in enterprise VoIP solutions |
| **Polycom** | 339 | Accord Networks | Video and voice network products for converged networks |
| **Sonus Networks** | 441 | Telecom Technologies, Inc. | Softswitch manufacturer |
| **Unisphere Networks** | Not disclosed | Broadsoft | Gateway, softswitch company |
| **VoIP Telecom** | 5 | NEX Telecom | Internet voice/data service provider |
| **Zhone Technologies** | Not disclosed | Xybridge | Softswitch company |

Source: iLocus.com "Global IP Telephony Market 2000/01."

arena—both on the technology and on the services sides. As with most volatile industries, communications is in a "weeding-out" phase. As a result, those companies with a sound business model, funding, and the technology to take services to the next level will survive. Table 4-2 lists the most notable acquisitions in 2001 and 2002. As you can see by the brevity of this list, clearly the boom in M&As has passed.

Table 4-3 puts the slowdown in telecom M&As in better perspective.

**Table 4-2. Telephony acquisitions, 2001 and 2002.**

| Buyer | Amount ($ Millions) | Company Acquired |
|---|---|---|
| Adir | 48.2 | Netspeak |
| C-Cor.net | Not disclosed | Aerotec Communications |
| Cisco | 181 | Allegro |
| Genuity | 106 | Integra |
| Level 3 | 50 | MacLeod USA |
| SS8 Networks | 45 | ADC Communications, Enhanced Services Division |
| Zhone | Not disclosed | Nortel's AccessNode |

**Table 4-3. Historical telecom M&A activity (U.S.).**

| Year | Announced Deals | Aggregate Value ($ Millions) |
|---|---|---|
| 1997 | 317 | 83,006 |
| 1998 | 388 | 260,925 |
| 1999 | 730 | 401,621 |
| 2000 | 909 | 251,350 |
| 2001 | 399 | 26,280 |
| 2002* | 213 | 12,556 |

*Year to date.
Source: Mergerstat. From Weber, "Lessons Learned from Last Year's M&As," *Telephony*, 8/27/01, http://currentissue.telephonyonline.com.

## Word from the Street

The interplay among and the huge corporate investments by companies like Cisco, AT&T, Comcast, Net2Phone, Liberty Media, AOL, and Time Warner are indicators of the value proposition for convergence, but what about Wall Street? Despite the economic blips that have plagued a host of sectors, it seems that when a company adds voice to its portfolio, investors listen. Vonage, a company that offers SIP-based VoIP solutions, completed $12 million in first-round financing in 2001, all of which came from prominent angel investors. These investments suggest the potential for sustained growth and opportunity for IP telephony products and services. (See Table 4-4.)

In Chapter 1, we examined the impact that participants from both the technology side and the service side have had on the economy. Overall business investments and profits in 1999 and 2000 were more robust than in the years that followed, but in the telecommunications industry investors still flock to new opportunities. Perhaps the rate at which investments occur will slow down from the frenetic pace of 2000, but they will not cease.

The analyst firm IDC totaled the major investments in IP telephony for 1999 and found that the total private and venture capital invested was in excess of $240 million, a figure that tripled in 2000. In fact, by March 2000, more than $875 million had been invested through just two deals: the Phone.com purchase of Onebox.com for $850 million and the HearMe acquisition of Audiotalk for $125 million.[2]

In 2001, the groundbreaking deals were AOL's purchase of Time Warner for $165 billion and Comcast's purchase of AT&T Broadband for $72 billion. Interestingly, until the AOL merger, the largest deal in history had been John Malone's sale of his cable company, TCI, to AT&T for $48 billion, signi-

**Table 4-4. Institutional investment activity in 2000.**

| Company | Investors | Amount Invested ($ Millions) |
|---|---|---|
| Rapid 5 Networks | Meritech Capital, Redpoint Ventures, US Venture Partners, Menlo Venture Partners, Bank of America's Venture Partners, Sumitomo Corporation | 70 |
| Dialpad.com | Serome Technology, CMGI@Ventures, Mokwon Assets Management, Citizens Capital, Sterling Payot | 67 |
| Eyak | UBS Capital Americas, me VC Drpaer Fisher Juvetson, Tudor Investment, Deutsche Banc Alex Brown, Siemens, iBasis, Venrock Associates, Zero Stage Capital, Bain & Company | 60 |
| EmpowerTel Networks | Goldman Sachs, Morgan Stanley, Sony Corporation, Chase Capital Partners/Access Technology Partners, Deutsche Banc Alex Brown, Anschutz Investment Company, Sandler Capital, Battery Ventures, InveStar Capital, TeleSoft Venture Partners | 54 |
| General Bandwidth | SBC Venture Capital, Sevin Rosen Funds, Sequoia Capital, Oak Investment Partners, Venrock Associates, Trellis Partners, CIT, HLM Management | 47 |
| Ubiquity | Celtic House Investment Partners, Alcatel, Cap Vest Equity Partners, JK$B Capital | 42 |
| CosmoCom | Intel Communications Fund, Marconi Ventures, Technology Crossover Ventures (TCV) | 40 |

| Company | Investors | Amount Invested ($ Millions) |
|---|---|---|
| **VocalData** | Austin Ventures, Trinity Ventures, Science Applications International, Chase Capital, Seed Capital Partners, Capital Southwest, Hickory Ventures | 32 |
| **Shoreline Networks** | JP Morgan Investment Management, Charter Growth Capital, Charter Ventures | 28 |
| **SS8 Networks** | Kleiner Perkins Caufield & Byers | 25 |
| **ipVerse** | Kleiner Perkins Caufield & Byers, Norwest Venture Partners, Battery Venture | 21.8 |
| **Pingtel** | Dain Rauschher Wessels, Intel Capital, St. Paul Venture Capital, Wind River | 12.7 |

*Source:* iLocus.com, "Global Telephony Market 2000/01."

fying the role that cable will play in bringing convergence to a commercial market.

In 2002, the most notable investment deal was the $500 million in funding made available to Level 3 Communications. The investors are Warren Buffett's company, Berkshire Hathaway; Legg Mason; and Longleaf Partners. Longleaf was the primary participant, investing $300 million. Berkshire Hathaway was a secondary participant, investing $100 million, giving the company junior subordinate notes that can be converted into equity. Legg Mason also invested $100 million. Perhaps the most interesting aspect of this deal is that Warren Buffett is a player. Buffett is long known for his reluctance to invest in technology ventures, and his involvement is a strong endorsement of the continuing role of telecommunications in the economy.

## The Holy Grail of Profitability

IP telephony is growing in functionality, diversity, and projected profitability. In fact, with so little in the tech sector a certainty these days, it's encouraging to see IP telephony product and service companies holding their own, with expectations for future earnings being eagerly assessed by industry analysts and investors. Projections are that worldwide IP telephony revenue will grow to $18.7 million in 2004 and that by then more than 90 percent of businesses with five hundred or more employees will be installing collaborative voice solutions. The enhanced services market is expected to exceed $12.6 billion in 2004, as well. These are all positive indicators as to how IP telephony will be embraced in the coming twelve to eighteen months. And in terms of usage, the estimates reflect equal growth opportunities. The industry anticipates that by 2004, traffic over IP networks will reach 135 billion minutes, racking up $19 billion in revenue.

### Revenue Projections

- Worldwide IP telephony revenue will grow from $500 million in 1999 to $18.7 billion in 2004 (106 percent CAGR growth). (IDC)
- Enhanced services revenue will increase from $270 million in 1999 to $12.6 billion in 2004. (Ovum)
- By the year 2002, nearly 30 percent of international phone traffic will be carried over data lines, up from only 0.2 percent this year. (Probe Research)
- 17 percent of large enterprises in the United States will begin implementing IP Telephony technology in 2000. (Yankee Group)
- By 2004, more than 90 percent of businesses with more than five hundred employees will be installing VoIP solutions. (Zona Research)

Convergence opportunities are impacting the strategies, initiatives, and investments within the telecommunications industry in an effort to create revenues by servicing the end user. Within the industry itself, service providers are delivering solutions to carriers and cable companies whose direct customer is the consumer. So far, this chapter has offered the market's viewpoint of voice from a management and financial perspective. The next section considers how convergent services will impact the end user at home and in a corporate setting. Chapter 5 examines the impact of convergence and IP telephony within the telecommunications industry itself.

## Convergence at Work: Benefits of IP Telephony in Business

The main advantages for corporations that adopt IP telephony are the cost-effective long-distance service and the availability of integrated network management solutions. With the technology maturing and convergent services becoming more pervasive, organizations are being presented with a host of collaborative solutions that can immediately impact the efficiency, productivity, and market reach of the company. From internal communications to customer service strategies, the myriad ways that convergence will appear within the business is startling. One aspect of this functionality can be seen in applications such as Click-to-Talk, a service being offered by Net2Phone and others that allows customers to speak with a sales representative by merely clicking an icon. Instant messaging that is VoIP-enabled within a company's Intranet is also a convenient but early use of this powerful technology. Chapter 5 examines how IP telephony is forcing the evolution of services, products, and markets as greater functionality and opportunities are conceived of and adopted by forward-thinking service providers.

The most immediate benefits for providers adopting IP telephony solutions are:

1. Cost-effective use of the network. IP telephony is a more economical alternative to PSTN. This is particularly true for global companies that are paying leased-line and high long distance charges between locations.

2. Better network utilization by making more efficient use of a company's available bandwidth.

3. Simplified and integrated network management for both voice and data.

4. Achievement of greater productivity by integrating operations that rely on voice, fax, or data. And, referring back to benefit no.1, they can respond to queries from any part of the world without incurring prohibitive costs.

## Adopting IP Telephony in the Enterprise

The major challenges to adoption of IP telephony in corporate settings are concerns about reliability and the extensive changes that must take place within the organization to incorporate a full rollout. Managers looking to benefit from IP telephony and convergence are concerned with quality, reliability, and investment issues. (Chapter 5 discusses these concerns in greater depth.) The tradeoff for some businesses is one of cost-effectiveness. I'm aware of organizations that have equipped their client companies with IP networks and voice solutions; they are not only passing the savings along but are creating an even more robust network system.

The conversion of existing PSTN and enterprise networks requires a significant investment in terms of training and adoption costs and also involves the risk of losing mission critical data if the migration isn't flawless. Choosing a technology vendor and service provider that can offer the functionality to fit your needs is key. Later in this book we discuss the strategies employed by service providers that are incorporating convergent services into their own portfolios and their approach to skittish customers.

Yet, despite these issues, convergence is clearly unstoppable; as services become more sophisticated and customers increasingly accustomed to greater personalization, the innate scaling ability of IP telephony will come into play. With this in mind, it makes sense for companies to consider a phased rollout of IP technology and convergent services.

---

Convergence is on an unstoppable path.

---

Right now, businesses are benefiting from the cost advantages associated with IP telephony. In the future, global organizations, as well as those that thrive on relationships with clients, will reap the benefits of converging voice, video, and data. Consider how a leading fund manager operates: negotiating with client businesses that want to purchase and trade, establishing a relationship with those companies whose stocks are included in the fund, and navigating the daily onslaught of financial data that act as a barometer of the fund's performance. These will become seamless activities that incorporate a personal approach with spot-on, real-time data.

## Adding Voice to Consumer Services

The opportunities to transform consumer behavior and to radically change consumer offerings have generated the greatest excitement in the telecom industry. Right now, we can see a range of benefits that IP telephony and convergence bring to such activities as online transactions, ecommerce, videoconferencing, messaging, and the distribution of media-rich content, but the possibilities are endless. As digital products infiltrate every aspect of consumer life, the ways that they can be used will increase exponentially. The technology has already progressed to the point that consumers using IP telephony through their phone or PC do so in a way that is becoming invisible to them. The limitations of the technology as far as equipment and usage are concerned will become a thing of the past.

While cost cutting might have once been the major attraction for those who decided to adopt IP telephony (particularly for international customers), the consumers' hunger for media-rich content and online conveniences has put convergence at the top of the agenda for customers around the world, and for the service providers that serve them. Chapter 6 introduces primary converged services and the impact they are having on both consumers and service providers. With the introduction of a host of new converged services, consumers have come to expect instantaneous service with a personal touch—and with good reason. Statistics on ecommerce transactions reveal that, while customers might browse on the Web, the majority prefer talking to a person when they place an order. When you think about the types of products and services being sold over the Internet—houses, cars, stock, luxury items—either via an auction or a retail site, the insecurity consumers experience is understandable. IP telephony adds a live person through click-to-talk solutions that have revolutionized customer relationship management (CRM) approaches.

### Ecommerce Without Voice

- 89 percent of people who "shop" on the Web buy on the phone.

- 62 percent of cybershoppers have aborted a transaction.
- 89 percent of computer users worry about transaction security.

## Bringing Convergence to Life: Voice Over IP

Voice Over IP (VoIP) is the primary driver in the development of convergent services because it is a single solution that is usable for all kinds of communications. The collaborative solutions that VoIP fosters are of value in any industry. In health care, for instance, doctors can not only review important medical data remotely, but actually converse with a patient from the remote location. With IP telephony's international appeal, think about what this type of functionality would mean to those in third-world countries.

---

"VoIP is the migration path to convergence."

—Joseph Aibinder, Director, VoIP Services, AT&T

---

Services that include advanced messaging, click-to-talk, voice portals, and voice Web are realities. How they will evolve as converged services to become a part of the enterprise and of the consumer mainstream will create a sea change in communications. Perhaps it is VoIP's ability to enhance the strengths of an individual company by making its network more dynamic that keeps the business press focused on voice technologies, identifying VoIP as a one of the top five technologies worth knowing about.[3] Early corporate adopters include industry giants such as Dow Chemical, which announced in June 2001 that it would initiate a VoIP system for its fifty thousand employees worldwide, connecting employees from Singapore to Brazil. The project will take about five years to complete, and it is estimated to cost the company $1 billion.

Like Dow, companies in a variety of industries are eager to adopt IP telephony. This is in part a result of the immediate cost savings and streamlined network management it brings, but probably just as important is the scalability VoIP solutions bring to the enterprise. No one can really say how business models and marketplaces will evolve over the next few years, but flexibility is a key aspect of VoIP, as is the ability to scale. The continual development of convergent services and improvements in voice and IP technologies will make it even more attractive. The analyst firm IDC has already gone on record pronouncing that "voice is *the* killer app in terms of telecommunications services."[4]

---

VoIP will change people's lives through increasingly personalized services.

---

## Market Forecasts for VoIP

The numbers speak for themselves. The opportunity VoIP offers to enterprise users and consumers is incredible. Even in this early stage of the market, VoIP traffic was responsible for a whopping 7.7 billion minutes in 2000, and that number is expected to increase to 500 billion by 2005. For consumers, voice will dramatically enhance the Web; from auctions to chat rooms to shopping online, voice boosts the value of existing services by a quantum leap. Next-generation business applications and new types of consumer services have caused a frenzy of activity among telephone service providers, Internet service providers (ISPs), and technology companies in all areas of high-tech.

The incumbent and emerging telephone carriers are investigating sending everything over IP networks because they can transmit anything digital over one inexpensive network, extending more elaborate services to their customers without incurring additional expenses. ISPs are also focusing on VoIP to increase the types of services they offer to their Web customers. Think instant messaging with voice and video!

Industry players know that VoIP will allow for services that will truly change people's lives. As the technology becomes more pervasive, we will see increasingly personalized services in the home. Teenage lines, where the time that calls are made is controlled and the ability to block certain numbers is enabled, are examples of this. Such a service is valuable for homes with multiple phone lines (and teens!). These services can further be applied to the Web. Instant messaging, chats, gaming, and similar activities all become much safer propositions. And if industry manufacturers and service providers have their way, you will have these services on any digital device: PDA, PC, laptop, or telephone.

## International Interest in IP Telephony

International interest in IP telephony is high but continues to focus on the inexpensive cost structure of the technology. In highly developed countries such as the United States and the United Kingdom, however, the draw is becoming future functionality, and several standards are being used to foster such advances. In less developed countries, the regulation and the use of IP telephony differ greatly.

For countries such as Nepal, where prices for international traffic are high, outgoing IP traffic is banned. Regulations governing incoming traffic are unclear, but such calls are harder to detect. In Nepal's case, PSTN traffic for incoming calls fell from 29 to 22 million minutes between 1998 and 1999, while outgoing traffic grew from 20 to 25 million minutes during the same time period. A strong contributor to the economies of these developing nations is the high price structure for telecommunications. Conversely, countries where prices for international calls are decreasing are experiencing greater competition among providers, and the view toward IP telephony is more dynamic.

The global state of IP telephony is made more complicated by the varying regulations and policies imposed on its use. In those countries where the regulators' agendas are more in line with the consumer, it would be politically incorrect to ban IP telephony. And in highly regulated countries where monopolies exist, a more restrictive approach is favored, one where the interests of regulators are in sync with those of the incumbent carrier. This is most often the case where the incumbent carrier is state owned. The International Telecommunications Union (ITU) has cited instances where carriers may restrict the range of licenses it offers depending on the political and economic position of the country at the time.

This being said, for countries that have a progressive approach to the Internet and telecommunications service, IP telephony makes a contribution to the national economy. In China, for instance, it is estimated that the IP telephony business will be worth $12 billion by 2004.

### Mother's Day Record

Mother's Day 2001 was a record day for VoIP. ITXC, a VoIP carrier, announced record-setting VoIP traffic for the United States and Mexico over its IP network. Without counting PC-to-phone traffic, Mexican traffic came in at over 4.2 million minutes and U.S. traffic was 5.7 million minutes on its networks alone. Of the U.S. calls, 96 percent were international and were made to more than two hundred different countries.[5]

In this chapter, we have discussed the market potential for IP telephony and convergent services, a potential that is sure to benefit professionals in telecommunications who are considering investing in convergence, as well as their investors and financial managers. Service providers and other industry participants can also begin to appreciate the revenue potential and market growth involved. Chapter 5 delves more deeply into the ramifications of IP telephony and the growing pervasiveness of convergent services on the industry itself and will particularly interest professionals in telecommunications, service providers, equipment manufacturers, and system integrators.

## Notes

1. Comcast Corporation, "AT&T Broadband to Merge with Comcast Corporation in $72 Billion Transaction," December 19, 2001.
2. Mark Winther, "Web Talk 2000: Market Forecast and Analysis," IDC, p. 20. Copyright 2000.
3. Ann Harrison, David Orenstein, and Robert Poe, "5 Technologies You Need to Know," *Business 2.0*, June 26, 2001.
4. Lee Doyle, Boom and Bust in Broadband Networks, IDC, 2001, p. 5.
5. Ron Archer, "US and Mexico Mother's Days Set All-Time VoIP Traffic Records," IP Telephony News, Pulver.com, May 14, 2001.

# CHAPTER FIVE

# The Power of Convergence:
## The Industry's Perspective

### The Evolution of Global IP Telephony

Like most of our current technologies, IP telephony began as a fascination of computer hobbyists around 1995 when transmitting voice messages from one PC user to another first became possible. At that time there were stringent requirements for making voice transmission work, including the need for both users to be logged on at the same time and for both computers to be multimedia PCs running identical software.

Internet telephony was first introduced in 1995. By 1996, IP technology had advanced to the point that voice messages originating on the public Internet could be communicated to a standard telephone. This became known as PC-to-Phone, and was an important development because it:

1. Increased the user base from tens of millions of PC users with multimedia PCs and IP telephony software to hundreds of millions of telephone and mobile phone users

2. Overcame the requirement for simultaneous connections between PC users

3. Created several new market opportunities for service providers and equipment manufacturers.

In 1997, opportunities in IP telephony gained the interest of the big telecom companies and vendors, and public telecom operators began offering phone-to-phone services over IP networks. Interest in phone-to-phone expanded around the world as international companies became aware of its market potential. A handful of key players emerged throughout 1996 and 1997 and investments began to heat up:

- In December 1996, Telecom Finland (which later became known as Sonera, a Nokia company) introduced its IP telephony initiative, known as MediaNet.

- Deutsche Telekom introduced its service in July 1997.

- In August 1997, the Japanese subsidiary of AT&T debuted IP telephony service between Tokyo, Osaka, and cities in thirty-six other countries; the service was accessed through a toll-free number.

Today, the majority of service providers and equipment vendors in this market have entered into international partnerships. The predominant use of IP telephony internationally is through prepaid calling cards, the result of licensing between U.S. service providers and international carriers. The prepaid calling card market is hot for all IP companies, and, while the draw of the cheap phone call is the motivation behind many international deals, it has resulted in an increase in awareness of IP technology. The largest target markets today are China and India.

While phone-to-phone helped educate end users and cultivate interest among telecommunications companies, advances in IP technology and the development of sophisticated voice services have enabled full communications convergence. This phenomenon, enabling the integration of complex voice and data over an IP network, has taken the industry by storm.

The opportunities for services that combine voice and data are continuously evolving. A live voice can be added to ecommerce transactions, benefiting both the business and its customers and altering the very nature of communications and the way individuals behave. Imagine taking a virtual tour of a home you're interested in buying while clicking to speak with a live person. The overall feeling of optimism about bringing convergence to life via IP has been summed up in a new industry acronym: XoIP—anything over IP! The possibilities are endless for the types of voice and data that will be transmitted and the applications that can be developed. In fact, anything that can be digitized can be shared over an IP network. As you read this book, IP telephony is already a viable alternative to circuit switch technology and is being applied to broadband, wireless, and all existing network systems. Criticism concerning quality loss and transmission reliability (i.e., will it really get there?) have plagued certain carriers and manufacturers, and perhaps have delayed the full integration of IP telephony into the commercial mainstream. I address these concerns later in the chapter and discuss how they relate to commercial and business adoption of IP networks, as well as how the current technology has resolved these quality and reliability issues.

## Types of IP Telephony Services

- PC-to-PC
- PC-to-phone

- Phone-to-PC
- Phone-to-phone / fax-to-fax
- PC-to-fax
- Text- and voice-enabled chat and email
- Unified messaging services (voice mail, fax-email, video-email, calendar, "follow-me")
- Web call centers
- Ecommerce applications
- Real-time audio/videoconferencing

## How IP Networks Work

IP networks make use of softswitch technology in which electronic transmissions (i.e, packets) are "chopped up" into packets of varying sizes. Each packet can carry a variety of digitized information, whether it be voice, video, multimedia, or text; with the aid of an address label, the packets are sent from one network node to another. The packets are transferred from one router to another in a way that makes the best use of the bandwidth made available on the network at the time of transmission. Rather than moving one behind the other, packets seek out pockets of bandwidth and move from node to node.

In contrast, circuit-switched technology maintains a direct and constant circuit though the network for the duration of the call, unnecessarily eating up bandwidth that ends up being both costly and time prohibitive. These bandwidth issues also limit the possible types of data transmission.

The most severe limitation of traditional circuit-switched technology is that the dedicated connection does not make optimal use of available bandwidth. On the pro side, sound quality is very high, and this is what diehard PSTN users cling to. As we have said, when a telephone call that uses circuit switch technology is in progress, the call holds onto a certain amount of bandwidth whether or not someone is actually speaking at the time. Even during moments of silence, the network is in use. With packet technology, the network is in use only when actual voices or data are being transmitted. This is accomplished by breaking up the transmission into packets that move dynamically along the network, making use of pockets of available bandwidth. In this way, the packets can avoid congested areas of the network. Packet switched technology is much more robust than circuit switch in that it uses its resources intelligently and can accommodate a much higher volume of transmissions.

## The Packet

The basic unit of IP technology is the "packet." A packet is to IP what an envelope is to postal service. Like an envelope, it is imprinted with a destination address and includes some type of information (i.e., data). Just as an envelope moves through the mail system and ends up being put into the mailbox, so too can data be sent over the network via a packet, which can be delivered anywhere in the world in a fraction of a second.

Current IP telephony is designed to add "intelligent" functionality to the network, such as caller identification (caller ID), integrated services, and unified messaging, that earlier versions did not support. In turn, formal standards, equipment, and regulations are now being designed to manage the boundless services supported by IP networks. The major difference between the past and the current versions of IP technology is the way they were linked to the PSTN. IP networks are able to integrate a diverse group of network systems by standardizing the connections or "gateways" linking myriad network systems. In the current MGCP standard, media gateways (MGs) perform simple encoding and decoding of analog voice signals, compression, and conversion to and from IP packets, and media gateway controllers

(MGCs) manage the signaling systems, ensuring PSTN connectivity.

What I find exciting about IP technology is the role it is playing in creating sophisticated services destined to change our personal and professional lives. Today, the direct benefits motivating carriers to throw away their circuit switches and adopt packet technology are:

1. The ability to achieve low-cost service

2. The integration of voice and data with comparable quality of service

3. The more effective use of bandwidth

## Standards and Regulations

### Regulations Governing IP Telephony

One of the primary reasons that equipment manufacturers and service providers are looking to introduce enhanced services that provide greater value is that the cost structure of the technology will soon be changing. Currently, two types of surcharges affect long-distance calls via the PSTN. These are access charges levied by local access providers and mandatory contributions to the universal service fund, which absorbs the cost of delivering service to remote areas. IP traffic was not included in the Telecommunications Act of 1996, which imposed fees and restrictions on regular telephone services that are subject to fees, taxes, and controlled cost structures. Since they are not covered by this law, IP service providers are able to offer dramatic cost savings. As I've mentioned before, inexpensive long-distance service is one of the main factors driving current interest in IP telephony;

however, it is the most simplistic utilization of this technology.

The lack of regulation regarding IP telephony is fleeting. At some point in the near future, the cost-effectiveness of IP will become less important as international regulations and tariffs change, and any business model focused solely around the cheap factor will fail.

## Standards for IP Telephony

As with many technologies that came before it, there is a standards war of sorts going on in the IP telephony industry. We've seen this type of confrontation take place with wireless technologies, open standards for such platforms as UNIX, software platforms, and so on. In the IP space, three standard-setting institutions dominate: the International Telecommunications Union (ITU), the Internet Engineering Task Force (IETF), and the European Telecommunications Standards Institute (ETSI). Adding to the confusion is the fact that IP networks can accommodate a variety of platforms, equipment, and applications. All this has made the selection of one overall standard a highly controversial issue. Another factor impacting the number of standards under development is the fact that different standards are needed for the different protocols that currently exist.

The three competing standards are ITU's H.323, IETF's SIP, and Media Gateway Control Protocol (MGCP). Some consider H.323 to be the most important standard for IP telephony opportunities, because it can support a multitude of services. While H.323 possesses many of the requirements for improved voice and data services, its use for more advanced services is uncertain because it was not designed with the ability to scale. As the Internet evolves, it's important that the standards have the ability to scale. Table

5-1 presents a number of proposed standards for IP tele-phony.

IETF's Session Initiation Protocol (SIP) and the Media Gateway Control Protocol (MGCP) are of prime importance to service providers, manufacturers, and vendors active in convergence. Some service providers, including Net2Phone, are working with all three standards in developing their technologies and services in order to capitalize on every service opportunity. Most industry participants are today banking on SIP, believing that this standard embodies the future of convergence.

One of telecom's most influential voices is Jeff Pulver, CEO of Pulver.com and organizer of the VON conferences, held all over the world. Pulver has applauded those companies that have invested in SIP, saying, "Show me a carrier with SIP support, and I'll show you someone who's looking to the future."[1]

Luckily, there is a level at which these standards complement each other, and they are being used interchangeably (SIP and MGCP often work together). This certainly lessens the confusion; more important, it keeps the momentum going as products, service, and application providers continue to innovate.

## Challenges and Solutions to Adopting IP Telephony

The most common criticism among consumers and corporate customers of IP telephony is that the technology itself needs further improvement. Quality-of-service (QoS) issues and the costs associated with rolling out IP networks are serious obstacles to its adoption. I remain (respectfully) amused by the second issue. What killer app didn't require similar investment? The major telcos and cable companies are slowly replacing their circuit switch technologies with

**Table 5-1. Proposed standards for IP telephony.**

| Standards Body | Protocol/ Standard | Function |
| --- | --- | --- |
| **International Telecommunications Union (ITU)** | H.323 V2 | Packet-based multimedia communications system |
| **ITU** | H.323 Annex D, E, F | Protocols for real-time fax, call connection, and single-use devices |
| **ITU** | H.320 | Narrow-band visual telephone systems and terminal equipment |
| **ITU** | H.245 | Control protocol for multimedia communications |
| **ITU** | H.248 | Gateway control protocol (corresponds to IETF's Megaco) |
| **ITU** | H.225.0 | Gatekeeper to gatekeeper; call signaling protocols and media stream packetization for multimedia |
| **Internet Engineering Task Force (IETF)** | Session Initiation Protocol (SIP) | Packet-based convergence communications system |
| **IETF** | SDP | Session description protocol |
| **IETF** | SAP | Session announcement protocol |
| **IETF** | RSVP | Prioritizes packet traffic |
| **IETF** | Megaco | Gateway control protocol |
| **IETF** | MPLS | Multiprotocol label switching |

softswitches and plan on adopting newer voice technologies in the next two years or so. Does this require time and money? Yes. Does it require smart management with strong strategic and operational skills and an equally passionate vision? You bet. But, in the end, having the ability to provide customers with richer services and methods of communication justifies the initial investment.

Concerns relating to reliability, throughput, sound quality, and security all involve QoS. These objections impact voice more than data transmission. The primary objection to IP telephony has been latency, which impacts delivery of the transmission and sound quality (i.e., jitter). In the initial packetization of voice or data, when the transmission is being digitized, a delay of on average one-tenth of a second occurs. This delay or latency causes the transmission to be choppy—creating the "jitter effect." IP telephony is improved by VoIP solutions that improve the packetization and transmission of voice and video. My finding, and that of my peers, is that IP telephony has approached carrier grade and has achieved "five nines" reliability. Of course, the quality of any product or service varies from vendor to vendor. Net-2Phone's technology has been praised for its quality and reliability by companies on both sides of the market, including AT&T and Cisco. Industry leaders, such as Net2Phone and Adir, invest in extensive research and are involved in strategic partnerships that offer access to the most advanced thinking on these issues. We feel that combining its own strengths with those of partners like Cisco and Netspeak has helped put Adir ahead of other technology companies.

## Deconstructing VoIP

VoIP allows for a multitude of interactions: bidding, buying, questioning, and manipulating data. Anywhere there is digitized information, the broadest range of interactions can occur. VoIP makes the IP network more functional. It is a solution—a service, if you will—that service providers themselves rely on to deliver convergent offerings.

### WHY VoIP?

- It's flexible. It works in all data environments, including broadband, wireless, and handheld.
- It will bring about value-added services: speech recognition, unified messaging, find me-follow me, Virtual Private Networks.
- It drives convergence.
- It makes use of a dynamic infrastructure.
- It's scalable and is primed to meet the evolving needs of a maturing marketplace.

VoIP converts voice into packets, so transmissions go into the network as voice and come out as packets with the opposite transformation on the other end. VoIP is embedded in the IP network and works with specific types of gateways or switches to allow for this conversion.

## Technology Drivers

The attributes of VoIP that lead industry analysts to characterize it as representing a paradigm shift in communications are these:

- *Accessibility.* VoIP allows for connections between myriad devices and multiple users (one example is videoconferencing that might make use of both wireline and wireless devices).

- *Viability.* It offers economic value that will only increase as inexpensive calls become a commodity and advanced services drive revenues.

- *Interoperability.* VoIP operates over a variety of platforms and can unify disparate network systems.

- *Reliability.* Advancements in VoIP and gateway technologies have reached a point where concerns regarding quality and reliability are becoming a thing of the past.

- *Availability.* VoIP allows for continuous, high-speed network access that is available to multiple users 24/7.

- *Scalability.* VoIP solutions are being developed with the future in mind. Ultimately, VoIP will be the most critical component in communications convergence. Over the next year or two, consumer needs will begin to mature, and convergence will have greater impact on the services and devices, making them even more futuristic. It is essential that the VoIP solutions in development can scale with these new trends and accommodate whatever the future brings.

These attributes are reinforced by VoIP's ability to manage extremely complex and diverse systems that address security, directories, and billing systems. Embedded in VoIP is the technology needed to ensure optimum quality and reliability.

## Market Drivers and Statistics

A number of market drivers are boosting the popularity of VoIP throughout the world; each will change in importance as the marketplace evolves over the next five years. Already discussed is the importance of two drivers: the deregulation of telecommunications markets and the cost savings from lower rates made possible by the cost-effective nature of IP networks. Right now, the deregulation of telecommunications service worldwide is advancing the use of VoIP, allowing service providers to expand globally. Countries in Western Europe and in Asia and along the Pacific Rim are quickly deregulating, as well, and are opening themselves up to a number of entrants, particularly U.S. companies, that are looking to gain a foothold in these regions. What analysts call "telecommunications liberalization"[2] is increasing competition between service providers and forcing traditional carriers to consider VoIP more seriously. The immediate benefits are lower operational costs and reduced customer churn.

However, the telecommunications industry is undergoing a "biological" change as it evolves to benefit from convergence. Service providers, carriers, cable operators, equipment vendors, and system integrators are reinventing themselves and now represent a maturing market . They are:

1. Expanding into less developed markets

2. Introducing more valuable services

3. Adopting broadband technologies

4. Replacing PSTN networks with IP networks

5. Including wireless technologies in their offerings

The introduction of value-added services, bringing broadband and wireless technologies into the mix, and the greater buildout of IP networks will lead to the greatest customer victory: convergence-based services that are simply not possible on traditional PSTN point-to-point telephone calls.

Replacing PSTNs with IP networks will have a tremendous impact on the pervasiveness of convergence, making the competitive landscape more dynamic and creating a sea change in how individuals communicate. This buildout is already under way; the VoIP industry has experienced dramatic growth over the past several years. In 1999, there were 595 million minutes of VoIP traffic. This number increased so that by the fourth quarter of 2000, there were an estimated 8,621 billion minutes of traffic over VoIP networks. Expectations are that VoIP traffic will reach 7 trillion minutes by 2006, yielding $374 billion in revenue.[3] (See Table 5-2.)

It's difficult to ascertain how sustainable this level of growth is. If we have learned anything about the economy, it is that market predictions are just that. In an effort to advance VoIP in a more strategic and focused manner, companies are sponsoring "trials" where different types and levels of service are market tested across a variety of regions.

## Why Broadband and Wireless Matter

Broadband enables higher-speed, data-heavy transmissions. This can directly increase the quality of voice and video. The

**Table 5-2. Traffic carried over VoIP.**

| Year | Units (Millions of Minutes) | Unit Growth Rate (%) | Revenues ($ Millions) | Revenue Growth Rate (%) |
|---|---|---|---|---|
| 1997 | 34.8 | — | 6.2 | — |
| 1998 | 268.6 | 671.84 | 60.7 | 879.03 |
| 1999 | 1,302 | 384.74 | 265.70 | 337.73 |
| 2000 | 18,533.01 | 1,323.43 | 2,650.22 | 897.45 |
| 2001 | 153,432.05 | 727.88 | 17,552.83 | 562.31 |
| 2002 | 767,676.76 | 400.34 | 71,232.60 | 305.82 |
| 2003 | 2,304,322.48 | 200.17 | 171,054.17 | 140.13 |
| 2004 | 4,610,584.32 | 100.08 | 276,635.06 | 61.72 |
| 2005 | 6,456,370.20 | 40.03 | 322,818.51 | 16.69 |
| 2006 | 7,490,258.84 | 16.01 | 374,512.94 | 16.01 |

Compound Annual Unit Growth Rate (CAGR), 1999-2006: 244.5%.
Compound Annual Revenue Growth Rate, 1999-2006: 181.8%.
*Source:* Frost & Sullivan.

combination of VoIP over cable/broadband technology will allow the transmission of the richest content and the most dynamic communication.

The high-speed Internet access enabled by broadband are up to thirty-five times faster than traditional dialup access. This type of speed allows customers to be more productive when using the Web and enables them to use richer media with interactive capabilities. This high-speed access is also expanding VoIP from the corporate world to that of consumers. IDC estimates that, by 2004, 50 percent of households in the United States will be using broadband.

Chapter 7 describes broadband cable technology more fully and assesses its role in expanding convergent services to consumers.

### VoIP at Home

The widespread adoption of broadband at home will cause a fundamental shift in ecommerce, Internet usage and behaviors, and the types of content delivered. These changes will result because broadband:

1. *Supports work at home.* High-speed access that was once the domain of the work world is now available at home, leveling the playing field between the two environments.

2. *Brings voice into the mix.* Broadband supports IP services and technologies such as VoIP, allowing for the delivery of richer media across a variety of platforms at any time.

3. *Allows for new applications and a greater variety of devices.* Broadband is multifunctional, operating on PCs, telephones, and handheld devices.

4. *Increases flexibility in multiple-PC homes.* Broadband allows for the concurrent use of multiple devices.

*Source:* IDC.

## The Role of Wireless Technology in Convergence

Wireless technology is reinventing the devices we use for communicating and gathering information; the physical constraints of landline connections are made obsolete. We are already seeing PDAs, cell phones, and other handheld devices imbued with greater functionality such as Internet access and advanced messaging. As convergent services become more complex and we reach the next level of value, handhelds will be endowed with a greater variety of applications and functions.

While wireless clearly makes VoIP accessible to a diverse group of devices, it also offers a solution to those regions where laying down physical networks is impractical or impossible. The potential for telecommunications companies to dominate global markets, for the reasons already discussed, is increased by the implications of wireless technology. Technology and service companies are establishing partnerships at a frenzied pace to make global inroads and to be the first to market in locales from Indonesia to Africa to the Pacific Rim. In June 2000, several companies, including British Telecom, Rogers Cantel, Ericsson, Lucent, Nortel Networks, Nokia, Telenor AS, and Telecom Italia Mobile, announced the formation of a focus group called 3G.IP and embarked on a strategy to develop and promote IP-based 3G wireless technologies globally.

## Convergence Makes Communications More Valuable

It's fair to say that the voice services have found an early adopter market among corporations. Enterprise solutions such as unified messaging, bill management, find me-follow-me messaging, Web-enabled call centers, distance learning, speech recognition, videoconferencing, and virtual private networks (VPNs) are driving corporate interest in IP telephony, in addition to the basic benefits of lower cost and easier network management.

For service providers, these applications are priced at a premium for the operational ease and greater productivity they bring to the organization. As these same services are being modified to serve the consumer market, the offerings that result will touch every part of our professional and personal lives. Imagine how live-person interaction via the Web will revolutionize everything from health care to law enforcement. And when customers experience the integration of wireless, PDA, and telephony devices—and are then able to include video in their communications—VoIP will have reached killer app status. Chapter 6 takes an in-depth look at the services available today that are poised to change the very nature of the way individuals communicate and share information.

## Notes

1. Jeff Childs, "confab Sees Slow, Steady Progress to VoIP," *EE Times,* July 30, 2001.
2. Frost & Sullivan report, "Voice Over Internet Protocol Services Market Forecast Update," #7401-61, 2000, pp. 3-4.
3. Ibid, pp. 24-25.

# CHAPTER SIX

# The Red Pill or the Blue?
## Ways Your World Has Changed

As in the surreal world portrayed in the movie *The Matrix,* customers in the real world don't know when unseen forces (e.g., VoIP) are at work behind the scenes managing their communications. The reality (that was the red pill, I think) is that voice instant messaging, online trading, unified messaging, and click-to-talk options may be VoIP powered services. But whether you know when or why VoIP is being used, the simple truth is that the world of communications has expanded the sheer number of ways, places, times, and modes in which information can be shared. And it is poised for even greater change as the industry itself evolves to hone business models, create new markets, and develop more intricate services.

The select services made possible by these applications are a result of a topsy-turvy time in the worlds of business, finance, and technology. Today, we are in an economy made up of savvy, ultraskeptical technologists and financiers. That's not necessarily a bad thing. For those of us who have dedicated a good part of our careers to advancing the tools of convergence, the continued ability of VoIP to create revenue is a validation of our efforts. However, as you read through this chapter, keep in mind that, in bringing these services to market, many companies and technologies have fallen by the wayside. Those companies and services that have been left standing have had to continually reinvent themselves or die. Reinvention might be an easy concept to understand, but it is quite difficult to implement and necessitates a Nostradamus-like ability to forecast market trends and a dedication to differentiation.

Assessing the maturity of a market in order to know when to promote your business model requires skill, patience, experience, and fortitude. Differentiation in your approaches, products, and services is key, particularly in saturated sectors like high tech and networking. Perhaps the Old School approach that investors now take toward technology, focusing on profitability, will encourage more companies throughout the industry to focus on reinventing themselves as necessary. Market share and subscriber growth, while feel-good metrics, have not proven to be accurate indicators of the future viability of a company, although they do reflect the sustainability of a new tech trend or service. Throughout this book, I've included information relating to both profitability and market share; taken together, these metrics give consumers, managers, and investors a broad view of the pervasive nature of VoIP.

This chapter will interest readers for different reasons. First, it lays out the movement within industry as technology and service companies compete to develop more integrated applications and cultivate a growth market through partnerships, licensing, and other collaborative deals. CEOs, COOs, CFOs, and other executives will find this aspect especially relevant as they continue to devise strategies for entering the convergence marketplace, either as a provider or an adopter. I then examine the market trends, as well as the influence each service currently has on user behavior, and the ways that market needs are evolving as convergent services become more widely adopted. Finally, and this will be of particular interest to managers and investors, I look at the benefits convergent services are bringing to the workplace right now, and the business and investment opportunities within each category of service.

Each service area can be thought of as a microcosm for the industry as a whole. My goal is to describe the influence convergent services currently have on global industry. They don't touch only the telecommunications industry but significantly impact businesses in finance, media, and the Internet as business models and as profit centers. By understanding the industry shifts, technology backbone, and adoption trends and by developing the ability to identify the leading companies, managers can devise better corporate strategies, and investors will be able to turn a discerning eye toward this sector as an investment opportunity with value and growth potential.

## Talk to Me: Changing the Scope of Communications

More and more, when you shop online or watch a television program that addresses the viewer (e.g., *America's Most Wanted*, the Home Shopping Network) and has a complementary Web site, there is a "click-to-talk" or "live person" option that makes viewing a real-time, high-tech experience with a personal touch. Voice-enabled instant messaging captures the same feel. While these are the most obvious representations of convergence for consumers, they are convergence in its most simplistic form. Just as it is a mistake to think that the scope of IP telephony is restricted to making cheap phone calls, it is similarly simplistic to assume that live-person access represents the full spectrum of communications convergence. In fact, the most sophisticated applications are being used as part of the backbone for financial services. These services handle millions of financial transactions daily in an arena where the data are constantly changing and truly every action causes a reaction.

Keep this in mind as your read this chapter. Extend your thinking from how people are using each of these services personally and professionally to ways such use will actually modify their behavior. It is this aspect that has spawned the popular notion that VoIP is an emerging killer app.

## Show Me the Money—IP Telephony as Money Maker

There are a handful of voice services currently being delivered to enterprise customers and consumers that are literally the profit centers of the IP telephony market. Long distance, international reseller, advanced messaging, and call management solutions are the primary categories of service that businesses and consumers are using at this moment. These are the "money" applications—the solutions that companies like Net2Phone, IBM, iBasis, and AT&T are banking on to create momentum for convergent services.

Live voice communications have been heralded as the launching pad for more interactive applications and as a platform for new revenue models. No longer are technology businesses to be governed by the word "free," relying on advertising revenue as their primary source of capital. Enhanced voice services offer greater value to consumers and command a comparable pricing structure. This business model has resonance among industry participants and customers.

The business platform that convergence stimulates is a much more sophisticated one, tied to products and services that offer a quantifiable degree of value and that are directed at particular market needs. Voice service providers are more attractive to advertisers because they target a specific market. It is important to note that, while advertising among these providers is estimated to increase, it is not the sole revenue stream or value proposition for these companies.

The free service model that helped to launch voice services by educating consumers is no longer viable. (Such a strategy was at first a blessing, but then a burden for Web businesses.) Subsidized by advertising, services such as Internet call waiting and virtual voice mail were bundled and distributed by companies like eVoice and Buzzme. Similarly, Tellme and Bevocal made free voice portal services available. Each of these companies has now adopted a pricing strategy commensurate with the value of the services being offered. The more customized, convenient, and robust the offering, the greater value it will hold for users. Of course, the trick is to determine which services, and in what combination, hold the most value for customers—and how to shift the dynamic to meet the economics of varying customer bases.

## The Market for Convergent Services

The primary value proposition of convergent services is to provide users with access to voice and data services through nontraditional means. The result is richer, more meaningful communications delivered with greater flexibility and convenience. Voice and data become interchangeable, as do the devices that typically deliver them to users. The underlying technologies that make convergent services possible are advanced enough and pervasive enough to be considered mature and are fueling the widespread adoption of voice services to carriers, enterprises, and consumers.

What is changing, however, are the business models deployed by service providers. The evolution of the business approaches and the pricing strategies emerging from the convergent services marketplace are reflected in the number of partnerships, mergers, and acquisitions within the industry itself. In order to extend their brand, create more valuable services, strengthen revenue streams, and flesh out their customer base, service providers are partnering with carriers, equipment makers, and even former competitors to define and lock down the convergent service arena. The growing sophistication of voice services and the desire to tap into new and varying audiences are important catalysts for industry participants to enter into some sort of strategic relationship. Partnership opportunities with companies like Seibel Systems combine voice and CRM solutions, increasing the value of these types of back-office solutions. Equipment vendors, systems integrators, and other broadband providers are entering into relationships with carriers and Web businesses that range from licensing agreements to outright acquisitions in order to provide the widest array of collaborative services. The first group benefits from such partnerships by improving their margins and offering more attractive products and bundling options, further diversifying their portfolio. The second group benefits by gaining access to larger audiences and by avoiding the initial investment associated with the adoption of new systems and solutions.

Within the convergent service community itself, providers are moving aggressively to differentiate their portfolios so that they are both commercially viable for today's user yet scalable to meet the growing and yet unknown needs of customers. In this way, service providers are distinguishing themselves from their competitors. More important, as they create pricing schemes appropriate to their customer segment, service providers will be better able to withstand pricing pressures in the telephony and data service markets.

In addition to creating diverse portfolios, analysts at

Frost & Sullivan believe that the greatest upside for service providers is in utilizing more fully the now-mature technologies that underlie voice services. Service providers can create customized service bundles that meet the individual needs of customers by expanding their use of text-to-speech, Voice XML, and speech recognition technologies. Because IP is an open standard, providers can make use of a variety of technologies to create customized and enhanced bundles that address the ongoing and future needs of customers. Imagine how such customization and convenience could benefit the investment community. Institutional and individual investors, investment bankers, money managers, and brokers would be able to access mission-critical information and conduct transactions from anywhere in the world via a phone or the Web. Customizing services to meet the individual needs of these customers, which would vary from firm to firm, would hold tremendous value for both the customer and the service provider.

## Market Drivers

Popular research supports my own experience regarding the factors that are creating change in voice communications and IP telephony. Investors, professionals in both technology and service companies, and the carriers themselves can benefit from an awareness of these drivers, which can lead to improvements in the popularity and economics of voice services.

### The Role of Industry Participants

The heated competition that exists among telecommunications service providers is fueled by the desire on the part of voice and data carriers to tap into one another's markets. Widespread deregulation, which reduced high calling rates, and the ensuing price wars among service providers and carriers increased these rivalries. As a result, service providers and carriers, whether voice or data, have suffered from high rates and churn as customers flip-flop between calling plans.

In Chapters 4 and 5, I discussed the many advantages of IP telephony and convergent services. These advantages include the following:

- Service providers have the ability to operate in a much more cost-effective way because of the nature of the IP network.

- IP networks are relatively inexpensive to build, particularly when compared to legacy systems; they operate on one open network and allow flexibility and scalability in order to accommodate richer services yet to be developed.

- IP telephony minimizes the cost and churn concerns that service providers have had to deal with when using traditional networks.

- The scalability of the network allows providers to differentiate their portfolios and to customize, bundle, and offer ever more sophisticated services that will improve customer retention and create more stabilized revenue streams.

- Since these richer voice and data services hold more value for customers, service providers will have more flexibility with their own pricing structure.

By incorporating enhanced voice services into their offerings, service providers have been able to improve several aspects of their overall business. They have moved away from an advertising-based, free-services model and developed pricing schemes appropriate to each customer base (enterprise or consumer). The ability to tap into new market niches has improved, as has customer retention, and companies have been able to diversify their portfolio of offerings to meet the needs of increasingly diverse groups of customers. All of these improvements have resulted in higher profit margins and greater shareholder value.

By aborting the free-service model that to an extent commoditized voice services, service providers have been able to further develop their own strengths, as well as to enter into partnerships that enabled greater diversification. The free-services model kept competitors focused on cheaper prices that centered around inconsequential service bundles, rather than on the more sophisticated services now available for an educated marketplace.

## The Role of Corporate Customers and Consumers

Another change brought about by the obsolescence of the free-services model is the realization among most service providers that the enterprise is their primary customer. While broadband and cable technology are making convergent services more appealing to individuals at home, businesses are benefiting greatly by the adoption of IP telephony.

The globalization of businesses and the increased complexity of the economy and the information it creates has led to a need for more sophisticated methods of communication. The urgency and volatility with which businesses operate each day make every transaction and every communication mission critical, and such operations become increasingly complex when key decision makers are in remote locations.

The financial underpinnings of any company can be severely compromised—from its stock price to inventory overages—if certain information cannot be communicated instantaneously when it is needed. The ubiquitous nature of convergent services has dramatically improved the communications, operations, and intellectual capital of enterprise customers.

In addition to improving internal operations and productivity, voice services are being used by companies as part of their strategy to improve customer relations and sales. And, because both the technology and service management can be outsourced to service providers or, in some cases, to full-service vendors, such as IBM Global Services and EDS, the up-front investment in training and upgrading is significantly minimized. Finally, the customization and bundling options that service providers offer hold tremendous value and appeal for both corporate customers and consumers.

From advanced messaging options to videoconferencing, convergent services can be designed specifically for an individual customer's needs at a particular moment. And these options can be rearranged at any given point because of the scalability, flexibility, and low cost of IP telephony. The higher degree of convenience and the immeasurable value that convergent services now represent to both enterprise and home users are important market drivers.

## The Red Pill: The Services That Are Changing Your World

The advent of converged voice and data has virtually guaranteed that communications—in whatever form—will never be the same. The very basis for our definition of communications has changed. Spoken words are transferred into data and data into spoken words that can be accessed by any number of devices: PC, TV, landline or wireless phone, or PDA. The convergence of voice and data will be the basis of communications going forward. And the more widely adopted

IP telephony becomes, the more pervasive IP technology at the network and platform levels will be. In this section, we examine the voice services that represent the new face of convergent communications.

## Advanced Messaging and Residential Call Management

Residential users with broadband capability have access to a number of call management services that providers bundle in any variety of ways. These include call waiting, caller ID, call forwarding, three-way calling, speed dialing, call-back, voicemail, inbound and outbound call blocking, and anonymous call rejection. The ability to provide these services over an IP network counters the argument that voice services are not comparable to those available on a traditional, circuit switch line. The value of these services is a combination of the cost-effectiveness, the flexibility, and the convenience that IP networks bring to users' ability to control all types of calls.

Internet call waiting, virtual voice mail, unified messaging, voice-mail-to-email, email by phone, and fax-to-email constitute advanced messaging services. Of these, and in consideration of growing broadband capabilities from the home or small office, it is likely that only unified messaging will have long-term market potential. For corporate use, a wider range of customized advanced messaging capabilities hold tremendous value for companies that are reliant on a field staff, on highly time sensitive data, or on mission-critical operations.

On the opposite end of the spectrum, Internet call waiting and voice mail are targeted at dialup modem users with a single telephone line—a market whose numbers are in serious decline and will decline even further with the increased penetration of broadband among residential users. Analysts believe that service providers offering Internet call waiting and voice mail will need to enter into partnerships that will serve to enhance these services, as well as create new packages and bundles (with Internet access or email services, for instance) in order to gain momentum in the market.

Unified messaging lets users consolidate incoming and outgoing messages from multiple platforms—fax, email, pager, and phone numbers—and access them through the phone and through the Web. The value of unified messaging draws from its status as an integrated solution, as opposed to an isolated service. It is a service that manages both voice and text in a variety of combinations, can be accessed over multiple devices, and can be customized to fit the personalized needs of each individual customer. Net2Phone, deltathree, and Voicenet are service providers active in the areas of advanced messaging and call management.

## Audio- and Videoconferencing

Less pervasive than the services previously discussed, audio- and videoconferencing have the most potential for businesses. Again, the cost-effective nature of IP networks, coupled with an enterprise's broadband capability (which is often not matched in the household market), makes these services attractive. The flexibility of the service itself is also a draw. Audioconferencing, which can be initiated via the Web or telephone, allows for the inclusion and exclusion of participants, file sharing, and even instant messaging capabilities. With the proliferation of broadband cable to the home, the dynamics of the marketplace are sure to change. (See Table 6-1.) The trick that service providers are always struggling with is to develop services that hold value and appeal for the consumer. Right now, conferencing capabilities are a natural for business. Translating that value for the individual consumer is the next step. Although this service is currently not offered on a large scale (as compared to messaging services,

**Table 6-1. Forecast demand for audioconferencing
services, 2000–2007.**

| Year | Demand for Audioconferencing Services (Millions of Minutes) | Penetration of IP-based Solutions |
|------|-------------------------------------------------------------|-----------------------------------|
| 2000 | 5,300  | —    |
| 2001 | 6,500  | 0.1  |
| 2002 | 7,600  | 2.5  |
| 2003 | 8,800  | 15.0 |
| 2004 | 10,100 | 30.0 |
| 2005 | 11,800 | 45.0 |
| 2006 | 13,700 | 60.0 |
| 2007 | 16,100 | 75.0 |

Note: All figures are rounded; the base year is 2000.
Source: Frost & Sullivan.

for example), it is included in many of the available service
bundles on the market. 3Cube and Telcopoint are two service providers that are actively promoting IP audioconferencing services to both the consumer and the corporate
market. Their price structure varies: 3Cube charges per min-
ute for its service, called PhoneCube, while Telcopoint, using
HearMe software, charges monthly for a specific number of
users. Table 6-2 presents forecast revenues derived from
business IP audioconferencing from 2000 to 2007.

IP videoconferencing services have become much more
popular over the past several years (see Table 6-3), offering
significant value to industries that rely on intellectual capital:
education, health care, media, finance, and sales, to name a
few. These services are gaining momentum due to improvements in the technology itself, customization of the service,
and the lower cost of IP services. With service providers
eager to add new offerings to their portfolio and the nature
of running global businesses, Frost & Sullivan estimates that
IP videoconferencing will account for 85 percent of all video-

**Table 6-2. Forecast revenues from business IP audioconferencing services, (U.S.), 2000–2007.**

| Year | IP Audioconferencing Services Revenue Forecast ($ Millions) | Growth (%) |
|---|---|---|
| 2000 | 0.00 | — |
| 2001 | 1.30 | — |
| 2002 | 36.10 | 2,676.92 |
| 2003 | 238.26 | 560.00 |
| 2004 | 519.57 | 118.07 |
| 2005 | 865.01 | 66.49 |
| 2006 | 1,272.10 | 47.06 |
| 2007 | 1,775.25 | 39.55 |
| CAGR* | | 674.70% |

*CAGR = Compound annual growth rate.
Note: All figures are rounded; the base year is 2000.
Source: Frost & Sullivan.

**Table 6-3. Forecast growth in videoconferencing services, 2000–2007.**

| Year | IP Videoconferencing Calls (%) |
|---|---|
| 2000 | 7 |
| 2001 | 11 |
| 2002 | 17 |
| 2003 | 30 |
| 2004 | 47 |
| 2005 | 80 |
| 2006 | 82 |
| 2007 | 85 |

Source: Frost & Sullivan.

**Table 6-4. Forecast revenues from business IP videoconferencing services (U.S.), 2000–2007.**

| Year | IP Videoconferencing Services Revenue Forecast ($ Millions) | Growth (%) |
|------|------------------------------------------------------------|------------|
| 2000 | 70    | —      |
| 2001 | 120   | 16.22  |
| 2002 | 220   | 15.12  |
| 2003 | 440   | 14.65  |
| 2004 | 800   | 15.86  |
| 2005 | 1,330 | 19.39  |
| 2006 | 2,020 | 23.89  |
| 2007 | 2,720 | 26.74  |
| CAGR |       | 69.65% |

*Note:* All figures are rounded; the base year is 2000.
*Source:* Frost & Sullivan.

conferencing calls in 2007, a significant increase over 2001, when 11 percent of all videoconferencing calls were IP-based.

The service providers most active in this service are Core-Express, DTVN Holdings, Sprint, and Wire One, each employing a different business model. CoreExpress delivers the service over the public Internet via the customer's T1 or T3 lines. Pricing varies depending on the number of sites that are video-enabled and on monthly usage (which is limited to a certain number of minutes). DTVN Holdings has incorporated a videoconferencing platform into its private IP network through its Video Intelligence Division. The company now offers low-cost, scalable, multipoint videoconferencing to companies of all sizes with competitive, on-demand pricing. Wire One is offering "Glowpoint Video" over IP services. Glowpoint is a network targeted at users who are beginning to move from ISDN to IP videoconferencing but who might not have the bandwidth or capabilities to support in-house IP services.

## Voice Portals

Voice portals enable users to navigate Web menus via commands spoken into an ordinary telephone or wireless phone, accessing content that is provided to them as either spoken responses or Web text. Advances in speech recognition and text-to-speech technologies, as well as the rigorous network management provided by VoIP, has catapulted voice portals into both the commercial and the enterprise worlds. Consumer voice portals deliver everything from weather forecasts to driving directions, stock quotes to movie schedules, and enable phone access to electronic messaging services. Customers can use voice portals to manage their portfolios, access subscription-based reports, or manipulate their personal account information. Businesses are using voice portals as a way to streamline their own internal operations. You can imagine how companies with large field staffs might benefit, or a how a transaction-based business could increase sales and improve customer retention through personalized service as users browse online and complete purchases over the telephone.

Voice portals are valuable because they present the most current information and knowledge, based on dynamically changing Web content, to users conveniently and speedily. The competitive edge in voice portal services lies with the underlying network infrastructure, as opposed to the nature of the content actually being delivered. Those networks that have five-nines reliability and a high degree of QoS will dominate this service area.

Like most IP telephony services, the voice portal market is still in flux—technologically and strategically. As the concept of free services is replaced by pricing models for services that hold greater value, new markets are being fleshed out both in the end-user segment and within the telco industry itself. Wireless carriers represent one of these newly formed markets that service providers are attacking.

Currently, there are three business models for delivering voice portal services:

1. Voice portal vendors offer services directly to business customers and consumers.

2. Voice portal vendors license their platform to other service providers (e.g., landline or wireless carriers).

3. Voice portal vendors host services provided by other service providers (i.e., carriers, enterprises).

Most of the major industry players fall into the first category of direct-to-consumer offerings. These companies have focused on increasing public awareness about the advantages of using voice portals, improving the reliability of the technology—particularly speech recognition and text-to-speech—and building scalability into both the services and the underlying technologies.

Service providers that offer voice portal solutions have a difficult balancing act; they are trying to attract more customers through the lure of free services even while they need to generate revenues. The heavy reliance of such services on R&D and the investment that R&D demands makes the free-services, ad-based model a tough one to sustain. Telcos are getting creative about revenue by bundling enhanced services that are customizable and competitively priced to both consumer and enterprise users. Table 6-5 provides data on the increasing use of voice portals worldwide.

## Advantages for End Users

Will voice portals make an increasingly complicated world of technology and information even more difficult to navigate?

**Table 6-5.  Voice portal services market: Minutes-of-use (MOU) breakdown by market segment (world).**

| Year | MOU: Free Services (Millions) | Growth (%) | MOU: Mobile VP (Millions) | Growth (%) | MOU: Enterprise (Millions) | Growth (%) |
|---|---|---|---|---|---|---|
| 2000 | 50 | — | 13 | — | 66 | — |
| 2001 | 800 | 1,500.0 | 1,315 | 9,865.5 | 7,500 | 11,263.6 |
| 2002 | 2,500 | 212.5 | 4,086 | 210.7 | 177,000 | 2,260.0 |
| 2003 | 7,500 | 200.0 | 13,041 | 219.1 | 442,500 | 150.0 |
| 2004 | 18,000 | 140.0 | 23,602 | 81.0 | 774,375 | 75.0 |
| 2005 | 35,800 | 98.9 | 35,240 | 49.3 | 929,250 | 20.0 |
| 2006 | 58,950 | 64.7 | 44,318 | 25.8 | 1,068,637 | 15.0 |
| 2007 | 84,750 | 43.8 | 53,799 | 21.4 | 1,175,501 | 10.0 |
| CAGR | | 189.3% | | 227.9% | | 304.8% |

Source: Frost & Sullivan.

There is that "blur" school of thought that considers many of these information-foisting technologies as disruptive, but, for most business people, solutions that deliver must-have information to remote locations are an important advantage. Voice portal services extend the wealth of information offered by the Web to users through the ubiquitous telephone. For business professionals who work remotely or travel frequently, this type of access and convenience is extremely attractive, providing constant and ever-present contact to job-related, mission-critical applications, as well as information resources that include corporate Intranets, personal messaging services, the latest stock quotes, and traffic reports.

Enterprise users that were early adopters of voice portal services realized immediate cost savings and improved productivity. Instead of managing large call centers, these businesses were able to use voice portals to deliver immediate help and information to their customers. In many cases, service providers license and manage the network and services for the enterprise, eliminating the need for complicated technology rollouts and reducing the burden on the business's financial and human resources.

Retailers are using voice portals as part of their customer relationship management (CRM) strategies to enhance point-of-sale experiences, increase sales, and improve customer retention. (I go into the benefits of voice services for online business operations later in this chapter.)

## Advantages for Service Providers

Advances in speech recognition, text-to-speech, and networking technologies have increased the quality of services like voice portals to a point where they are carrier grade and now have more mass-market appeal.

Certainly, carriers and service providers view a large part of their market as being made up of consumers. As business models in this sector evolve and the technology matures, there is a strong appeal to both the consumer and the corporate marketplaces for voice services, in a variety of forms. Bundled, customized services have become the focal point for service providers looking to create a steady revenue stream and to attract and retain both corporate and individual customers. Providers that offer voice portal services using an IP network can achieve these strategic goals thanks to the cost-effective nature of IP technology compared to circuit switch, the ubiquitous characteristics of IP, and the ability of IP technology to enable scalable providers to differentiate and customize their portfolios of service.

The importance of expanding service portfolios is both market and profit related. Obviously, enhanced services are going to gain the interest of a broader clientele; more important, though, as providers move away from an advertising-based revenue model and must transition their customers from free-of-charge services to fee-based services, the services in question need to hold greater value. By bundling services and customizing them for the particular needs of an individual or corporation, providers can achieve this greater value. The proliferation of IP networks through technologies, such as cable, will, in turn, create a more robust environment for the convergence of voice and data and for the services that convergence engenders.

Service providers in all areas of voice services—carriers as well as wireless and data service providers and including voice portals—are entering into strategic partnerships and joint ventures in an effort to strengthen their portfolios.

## Minutes of Use and Revenue Forecasts by Market Segment

The voice portal market is developing around three service categories: advertisement-based free services; paid consumer services; and customized corporate services. Earlier in this chapter, we looked at how business models in the voice services marketplace are evolving to create sustainable revenue streams and to minimize the risk associated with free services. Like other voice services, enterprise use of voice portals is emerging as a growing segment, one that is scalable and offers a value proposition that ensures revenue opportunity.

The two primary reasons for the growth in the enterprise segment over that of the consumer market is the providers' ability to offer increasingly customized and complex services and the growing demand by enterprises to incorporate voice portals into their operations and own service offerings. Analysts expect enterprise voice portal services to significantly exceed revenues generated through consumer services (see Table 6-6).

The numbers for voice Web services that include voice portals as well as other services that rely on speech recognition and text-to-speech are even more impressive and show that the services are gaining penetration quickly (see Table 6-7). In addition to voice portals, voice Web services comprise voice-activated dialing, voice-accessed calendar, voice accessed directory assistance, and email reader.

Outsourcing voice Web services from other service providers has become a viable strategy for carriers and enterprises eager to add these options to their own portfolio and operations. As we continue to examine the dual audience for IP telephony, service providers and end users, take special note of the revenues being generated within the industry through outsourcing (see Table 6-8). The growth in revenue forecasts is being driven by the increased complexity of services, greater customization of services and bundles, and the cost benefits of IP, which will continue to fuel competition and further price decreases in the telecommunications industry.

*(text continues on page 112)*

**Table 6-6. Voice portal services market: world revenues by market segment.**

| Year | Revenues: Free Services ($ Million) | Growth (%) | Revenues: Mobile VP ($ Million) | Growth (%) | Revenues: Enterprise ($ Million) | Growth (%) |
|---|---|---|---|---|---|---|
| 2000 | 0.5 | — | 2.2 | — | 8.9 | — |
| 2001 | 4.0 | 661.9 | 106.8 | 4,649.0 | 761.7 | 84,22.7 |
| 2002 | 8.6 | 115.6 | 183.0 | 71.5 | 10,694.5 | 1,304.0 |
| 2003 | 15.8 | 82.6 | 404.1 | 120.8 | 21,649.4 | 102.4 |
| 2004 | 34.2 | 117.1 | 541.9 | 34.1 | 33,886.9 | 56.5 |
| 2005 | 60.9 | 78.0 | 643.5 | 18.7 | 36,698.5 | 8.3 |
| 2006 | 100.2 | 64.7 | 717.1 | 11.4 | 37,953.5 | 3.4 |
| 2007 | 115.3 | 15.0 | 760.8 | 6.1 | 38,993.5 | 2.7 |
| CAGR | | 116.0% | | 129.8% | | 229.5% |

Note: All figures are rounded; the base year is 2000.
Source: Frost & Sullivan.

**Table 6-7. Revenues from consumer voice Web services (U.S.).**

| Year | Mobile Services ($ Millions) | Growth (%) | Free Services ($ Millions) | Growth (%) | Web Portal Services ($ Millions) | Growth Rate |
|---|---|---|---|---|---|---|
| 2000 | 3.4 | — | 0.00 | — | 0.00 | — |
| 2001 | 177.5 | 5,192.5 | 4.00 | 661.9 | 9.00 | — |
| 2002 | 326.7 | 84.0 | 8.63 | 115.63 | 23.30 | 158.75 |
| 2003 | 591.2 | 81.0 | 15.75 | 82.61 | 80.72 | 246.50 |
| 2004 | 755.7 | 27.8 | 34.20 | 117.14 | 205.95 | 155.15 |
| 2005 | 1,026.3 | 35.8 | 60.86 | 77.95 | 486.56 | 136.25 |
| 2006 | 1,314.9 | 28.1 | 100.22 | 64.66 | 689.70 | 41.75 |
| 2007 | 1,630.6 | 24.0 | 115.26 | 15.01 | 736.49 | 6.79 |
| CAGR | | 142.0% | | 116.00% | | 857.25% |

Note: All figures are rounded; the base year is 2000.
Source: Frost & Sullivan.

**Table 6-8. Revenue forecasts for voice Web services outsourced by carriers, enterprises, and voice portals (U.S.).**

| Year | Outsourcing Revenues ($ Millions) | Growth |
|------|-----------------------------------|--------|
| 2000 | 4.6 | — |
| 2001 | 141.43 | 2,971.3 |
| 2002 | 1,519.39 | 974.31 |
| 2003 | 4,799.69 | 215.9 |
| 2004 | 8,236.79 | 71.61 |
| 2005 | 9,566.72 | 16.15 |
| 2006 | 12,033.51 | 25.79 |
| 2007 | 13,520.75 | 12.36 |
| CAGR | | 212.89% |

Source: Frost & Sullivan.

In this chapter, we presented a comprehensive overview of the most promising services in IP telephony, as well as figures on customer penetration. Chapter 7 introduces cable to the mix. Cable IP telephony holds great potential for advancing the level of services offered and for distributing these services directly into the home.

# CHAPTER SEVEN

# "Someone Will Be There Between Nine and Five . . .":
## Broadband/Cable

You can bet that when RCA president and NBC broadcast pioneer David Sarnoff introduced television to an eager America at the 1939 World's Fair, he did not imagine how far the technology would grow, or the power television would soon have when coupled with cable technology. As they did with television, cable networks have now also magnified the reach of the Internet. This chapter delivers a broad overview of the impact of cable on the Internet through IP cable telephony, the effect broadband cable will have on these services, the strategies that participants are adopting to effectively compete in this marketspace, and the profit potential for IP cable telephony.

## Cable Will Be King

Cable customers have access to a broad range of services, from high-speed Internet to digital video to Web TV, and now cable telephony has been added to the mix. And with these services comes an ever-increasing number of new subscribers. High-speed Internet access is available to more than sixty million households in the United States, and more than 1.3 million residential telephone customers receive their telephone service from cable companies, with seventy thousand new subscribers added each month.[1] AT&T Comcast Corporation, Cox Communications, and Cablevision are among the service provider leaders in the cable industry, and they do so because they can offer savings of 10 percent, 20 percent, and even 50 percent over that of the incumbent telcos. By adding telephony to their portfolio, cable operators, or multiple systems operators (MSOs), can find new customers in the residential market, solidifying the price structure of their services through bundling and other customized options. MSOs, led by Cox Communications and AT&T Comcast, are investing heavily in residential cable telephony. Cox's residential telephony subscribers are growing at a rate of 118 percent annually, and AT&T Comcast currently serves more than 850,000 residential customers through its cable operations.[2]

There is an excellent reason why MSOs are getting into the telephony business: the number of cable customers is growing at incredible rates. In addition, cable subscribers have an insatiable appetite for high-speed digital services. The more you can offer, the more services they are going to want.

Cable modem customers grew from 600,000 households in 1999 to 7 million in 2002, while digital cable subscribers expanded from 1.5 to 7 million U.S. households. Though still in its early stages, IP cable telephony services expanded its subscriber base from 198,000 in 1999 to 2 million in 2002, according to the National Cable & Telecommunications Association (NCTA).

**Table 7-1. 2001 cable industry statistics.**

| | |
|---|---|
| Basic cable households | 72,958,180 |
| Cable penetration of TV households | 69.2 percent |
| Pay cable units | 51,610,000 |
| Digital cable subscribers | 13,700,000 |
| Cable modem subscribers | 6,400,000 |
| Cable delivered residential telephone subscribers | 1,500,000 |
| Cable industry upgrade expenditures | $14 billion |
| Annual cable revenue | $48 billion |

*Sources:* NCTA, www.ncta.com.

Fueling residential users' desire for cable telephony and other high-speed services is the increased penetration of broadband. Currently, there are about 69 million U.S. households with cable access; 12 percent of these, or one in eight, have broadband capabilities.[3] With broadband access becoming more pervasive among cable customers, and given the technological advances that have made IP networks and VoIP carrier grade, cable telephony is poised to be one of the three primary services being offered by MSOs and sought after by both residential and corporate customers.

### Say Hello to Hollywood

On August 16, 2001, five of the entertainment industry's most powerful film studios announced that they would launch a movie download service accessible only to broadband Internet subscribers. The fee-based service will make feature films available for download and viewing at the time they are released to pay-per-view audiences. The studios—Sony, MGM, Paramount, Warner, and Universal—sparked a flurry of activity among the other major studios. With the initial announcement came "me-too" statements from Disney and Fox. In addition to the convenience and multiple-viewing aspect of the initiative (movies will have a thirty-day life on the target hard drive), the long-term value is that movies will remain permanently accessible online, eventually creating a massive library of titles that can be viewed on demand at any time from any device with a broadband connection.[4]

## Bringing IP to Cable

Until recently, cable telephony has made use of traditional circuit switch technology, requiring those MSOs that offered telephony to invest heavily in upgrading their switches to carry digital and other advanced services. Circuit switch technology in cable operates the same way that it does in telephony, with a circuit or path making itself available on a per-call basis, in a linear fashion. However, as with telephone service providers, MSOs have begun to embrace IP technology to varying degrees for its obvious benefits of cost effectiveness, network integration, and bandwidth optimization. And, like the telcos, MSOs are beginning to invest in their IP infrastructures. While MSOs previously focused heavily on developing their circuit switch infrastructure, resources are now being redirected toward the purchase and development of IP networks and VoIP solutions. The reason for this strategy is threefold:

1. Huge capital investments are required to purchase and install switches, while IP networks with VoIP represent an incremental expense.

2. Unlike the complex processes and expensive equipment needed to upgrade circuit switch technology to meet changing service needs, VoIP solutions can be upgraded expeditiously and seamlessly to facilitate software changes, upgrades, or additions to service packages.

3. The interoperable nature of IP networks enables it to accommodate a variety of equipment and services.

MSOs benefit from using IP technology rather than circuit switches for the same reasons that telecommunications providers do: IP networks are integrated, cost effective, and scalable. Circuit switch technology is effective but not efficient; it consumes more dedicated bandwidth than IP, making it more expensive to deliver and upgrade.

## Standards for IP Cable Telephony

Equipment vendors in the IP cable telephony market supply the cable modem termination systems (CMTS) technology that makes cable telephony service possible. In fact, Frost & Sullivan characterizes CMTS as the "engine of an MSO's cable telephony service."[5] The equipment vendors that dominate this market are Arris Interactive, ADC, and Tellabs. These vendors are now using the most current protocols for IP cable telephony: Data Over Cable System Interface Specifications (DOCSIS) 1.0 and 1.1. (DOCSIS 2.0 was recently completed.) The industry is unanimously moving toward 1.1, a transition that has the MSOs waiting for complete adoption of 1.1 by all major industry players.

DOCSIS is an industry standard developed by CableLabs, the standards and testing body for cable modems and CMTS equipment. DOCSIS defines and prioritizes packet flow over HFC cable networks. DOCSIS 1.1 is the prerequisite for PacketCable software that duplicates circuit switch technology, but with one important difference: it maps out the entire route, rather than just point-to-point transfers. DOCSIS 1.1 includes the QoS features needed to ensure that calls placed over IP cable are clear, synchronized, and complete. Those MSOs that haven't yet invested in circuit switched technologies are instead focusing solely on IP. Charter Communications explained its approach to the NCTA as "being in the middle of deploying high-speed data services using the DOCSIS platform across the majority of the company." Charter is leveraging the "DOCSIS platform for other services, and IP telephony fits into that space very well."[6]

Like their MSO counterparts, CMTS vendors are partnering with equipment manufacturers and IP service providers like Cisco, Nuera, and Sonus to IP-enable their own products. The number of CMTS companies that are upgrading to DOCSIS 1.1 is increasing; however, fully developed softswitch applications for cable are just now becoming available. The availability of softswitch applications and the transition to DOCSIS 1.1 from 1.0 are two critical technical issues impacting the wide-scale rollout of IP cable telephony among MSOs.

### CMTS Activity

- Arris Interactive's Cornerstone CMTS router is being deployed on a small scale and is one of the leading solutions being tested for DOCSIS 1.1 qualification. It already has 1.0 qualification.
- ADC's Homeworx solution is widely deployed for circuit-switched cable telephony. Its more current product, Cuda 12000 IP Access Switch, enables IP cable telephony and is being used in more than forty trials, including some by AT&T Broadband.
- Motorola is partnering with Convergent Networks to integrate its ICServiceWorks softswitch into VoIP solutions.

## Selling IP Cable Telephony

IP cable telephony is the transmission of telephony services over cable lines that make use of IP networks; as such, it represents complete convergence. For consumers, cable represents a communications lifeline—all media, entertainment, and connectivity are transmitted over their cable line. For telephony service providers and MSOs, cable penetration opens up a broader market of users.

Earlier in this book we noted that the two categories of telecommunications service providers—those that provide voice and those that provide data—have begun to enter into partnerships that make use of each partner's core competencies and that offer all of the services made possible by VoIP. The same is true for MSOs. MSOs have come to realize that the richer the services, the more attractive they are to subscribers and the more robust their pricing structure will become. IP cable telephony with VoIP provides MSOs with the opportunity to develop a whole array of new services, revenue streams, and subscriber bases, which they will use to compete with the telcos. More and more, the cable industry is evolving to include partnerships between cable companies and telcos, media companies, equipment manufacturers, and ISPs in an effort to leverage the individual strengths of each partner.

Until 1996, cable and telephony providers offered their services independent of each other. The deregulation that changed the landscape for telco providers did the same for MSOs, and the race for convergence took on a renewed urgency. In addition to benefiting from the Telecommunications Act of 1996, MSOs benefited from a recent appellate court decision designed to ease limitations on the types of partnerships entered into by media giants such as AOL/Time Warner, Viacom, and Walt Disney. The February 19, 2002, ruling requires that the government carefully consider any limitations it is contemplating regarding the number of stations a network can own and completely tosses out the regulation prohibiting cable operators from owning television stations. In addition to facilitating wider distribution of voice, video, and data-rich content, the ruling has created the context for full convergence. As cable, telcos, media, and broadcast companies begin to partner and merge, the devices we use to communicate will become interchangeable and the content of the information shared increasingly multifaceted.

IP networks make MSO expansion into other service areas both cost-effective and a strategy for profitability. Another benefit for MSOs that move to IP cable telephony is reduced customer churn as fewer users go to DSL providers.

Strengthening the market for IP cable telephony is not without its challenges, however. Telephony services are competing with video-on-demand and other premier offerings and have often been relegated to second-line households. The goal for MSOs is to penetrate the primary line or "lifeline" marketplace, as well as to further develop the enterprise market. These strategies are discussed in further detail in the next section.

## Making IP Cable Telephony a Primary Service

In addition to the technical challenges MSOs face in rolling out IP cable telephony, they also have to compete with other high-speed cable services, such as digital television and video-on-demand. Making IP cable telephony services a primary-line service and fleshing out untapped markets are two mandates for MSOs committed to offering IP-based cable services.

Right now, IP cable services are not what is known as a "stand-alone service"; that is, they need to be bundled with many other services in order to appeal to subscribers. Industry analysts view voice as part of a triple play for MSOs in which voice, video-on-demand, and high-speed data are all made available to subscribers. It is a strong business model that guarantees price insensitivity on the part of subscribers, but it is also a competitive strategy that requires attracting customers from regional Bell operating companies (RBOCs) and Internet service providers (ISPs).

There are a number of factors that make this "hat trick" model difficult to deploy: the technical readiness of IP cable networks (discussed later in this chapter) and the practice of open access, through which MSOs offer customers who use high-speed data services their choice of ISP. Open access was a condition imposed by the FCC when it approved the AOL/Time Warner merger, and it is being adopted by MSOs wary of future anticompetitive rulings. Open access is a tradeoff; it has opened up the playing field a bit and resulted in partnerships between MSOs and ISPs to develop new services and advanced infrastructures that further support the delivery of high-speed data.

In looking for new customers, MSOs have identified small and medium-size businesses as potentially lucrative targets. Only 25 percent of such companies have cable access, compared to 70 percent of U.S. households. Small and medium-size businesses can use cable for data services that include Internet and Intranet access, Web hosting, virtual private networks, voice, and videoconferencing. To engage this market, MSOs need to present themselves as full-service and telephony providers, as opposed to just cable television service providers. In this regard, some of the larger MSOs— AT&T Comcast, Time Warner, and Cox—have created distinct business units designed to attract the enterprise market.

Partnerships and mergers between cable operations and both media and telecommunications companies support the belief that IP cable telephony is a burgeoning profit center that facilitates the advancement of many types of communications over multiple devices and supports a strong and growing subscriber base. Dating back to 1998, when AT&T began acquiring and partnering with cable operations, from its acquisition of John Malone's TCI to its merger with Comcast, the allure of combining alternative modes of connectivity has been clear. In 2001 and 2002, acquisitions and partnerships have been on the rise: AOL's merger with Time Warner, Comcast's purchase of AT&T Broadband, and Cisco's partnership with Time Warner and MediaOne were designed to ensure that a cable infrastructure for IP service was in place. These are the types of deals that, even in a soft economy, signify confidence among investors and industry participants.

### MSO Deals and Partnerships

- Motorola and Nortel Networks entered into a nonexclusive agreement to create and deliver VoIP solutions for broadband cable providers. The partnership leverages Nortel's experience in establishing large networks that can handle voice and data traffic with Motorola's leadership in IP cable access. (2/02)

- Thomson Multimedia will deliver one million DOCSIS 1.1 cable modems to AT&T Broadband by 2004. (1/02)

- Cox Communications chose Cisco's routers for its planned network expansion, creating a nationwide IP backbone. (1/02)

- ComMatch is collaborating with IBM to supply DOCSIS-based IP telephony solutions to cable TV operators. IBM will use ComMatch's VoIP solution as part of its own complete integrated solutions. (11/01)

- IP Unity partnered with Gallery IP to provide an integrated package to carriers that will allow the delivery of IP cable telephony services to business and residential subscribers. The partnership leverages IP Unity's server technology and applications with Gallery IP's softswitch technology. (10/01)

- Mitel acquired e-smith, Inc., a software developer for open-source networks that serves small and medium businesses. The acquisition will enhance the market potential for Mitel's own IP solution, March Networks 3100. Further, by combining e-smith's products with the March Networks product suite, Mitel will be able to deliver a complete telecom and networking package that is effectively a "plug and play" application. (7/01)

## It's All About Broadband: The Prerequisite for IP Cable Telephony

When you look at the market potential for IP cable telephony, it makes sense to first establish the "broadband readiness" of the marketplace. According to eMarketer, the United States leads the world in broadband readiness.[7] Broadband penetration in the United States will reach ninety million households by 2004, according to forecasts by Allied Business Intelligence and by Ovum. Currently, approximately forty million households have broadband access. These numbers include both DSL and cable broadband subscribers. However, in most parts of the world, cable has taken a strong lead over DSL. According to eMarketer, the primary reason for this is that the introduction of services via DSL has been slow. Also, MSOs know that DSL technology is limited. With broadband, high-speed data, voice, telephony, and video services can be bundled and offered in a variety of ways to IP cable customers.

The technological advances made by communications companies—both equipment and service providers—in the United States has contributed to making it the largest broadband market in the world. The company eMarketer has estimated that more than thirty million households (29 percent) will have broadband access in 2004 (as compared to Ovum's estimate of forty-one million); of these thirty million, 85 percent will connect to the Internet via either cable modem or DSL, in almost equal numbers. Table 7-2 breaks down eMar-

**Table 7-2. U.S. households with broadband access (millions).**

| | 2000 | 2001 | 2002 | 2003 | 2004 |
|---|---|---|---|---|---|
| Cable | 3.2 | 5.8 | 8.9 | 11.1 | 13.3 |
| DSL | 1.5 | 3.4 | 6.5 | 9.1 | 13.1 |
| Other | 0.2 | 0.6 | 1.5 | 2.8 | 4.6 |
| Broadband households | 4.9 | 9.9 | 16.9 | 23.0 | 31.0 |
| Dialup | 40.8 | 46.7 | 49.9 | 48.1 | 45.6 |
| All online households | 45.7 | 56.6 | 66.8 | 71.1 | 76.6 |

*Source:* eMarketer.

keter's forecasts. (It is interesting to note that this industry is in flux, and comparative market forecasts among analysts differ by as much as 10 to 15 percent in some cases.)

## How Industry Is Developing the Market for IP Cable Telephony

The two major service providers in this market are AT&T, now strengthened by its merger with Comcast, and Cox Communications. Of the two, AT&T is believed to account for approximately half of all U.S. cable telephony subscribers. With Comcast in its corner, AT&T chairman Mike Armstrong was reported as saying that the partnership was "a great leap forward . . . bringing greater choice in affordable broadband video, voice, and data services to even more American homes."[8] Table 7-3 identifies the leading U.S. MSOs.

## Business Models, Strategies, and Profitability

MSOs that are aiming at adopting IP cable telephony and thereby achieving full convergence have embraced one of

**Table 7-3. Leading MSOs.**

| Leading US MSOs | Household (millions) |
|---|---|
| AT&T Broadband | 13,750,000 |
| Time Warner | 12,654,000 |
| Comcast | 8,437,000 |
| Charter Communications | 6,970,100 |
| Cox Communications | 6,206,700 |
| Adelphia | 5,693,000 |
| Cablevision Systems Corporation | 2,988,600 |
| Mediacon LLC | 1,585,000 |
| Insight Communications | 1,361,300 |
| CableOne | 754,900 |
| All others | 3,422,300 |
| Total cable markets | 63,822,900 |

*Source:* NCTA, ncta.com.

two strategies: offering IP cable telephony now through trials in select markets or prototyping internally now and waiting until IP matures before initiating a full rollout. As the telcos have found, replacing circuit switch lines with IP is an expensive proposition, so MSOs are using IP for their new lines while phasing out existing circuit switch lines.

Time Warner Cable, AT&T Comcast, Charter Communications, and Adelphia are just a few of the MSOs that are already conducting real VoIP trials in select markets. Typically, the trials are being run on a very small scale, with only a few hundred households participating. In 2001, Time Warner conducted two trials utilizing its Line Runner service; each trial involved one thousand households. The service is currently being offered to Time Warner's RoadRunner customers; the IP line is intended as a second line or a fax line for the home or home office.

The primary objectives of these trials are to test the market and to gain experience in providing telephony services, a new playing field for cable providers. By integrating IP into their cable networks to enhance second-line services, MSOs are building the experience they will need when IP cable telephony becomes a lifeline or a primary-line service. Once IP cable telephony matures and MSOs begin offering lifeline service, the transition should be seamless and the service a long-term value proposition for MSOs.

Those MSOs and telcos that are waiting for IP to mature before rolling out full IP cable telephony services are envisioning a business model of primary-line service. According to Frost & Sullivan, building a business around lifeline services is a lucrative business model compared to second-line opportunities. Primary-line service has unlimited potential in terms of the services themselves, as well as bundling and pricing opportunities. For MSOs like AT&T Broadband, trials provide good market feedback, but their primary strategy is to optimize existing circuit switch infrastructure and then to migrate to IP when the competition dictates. The downside of this strategy is the possible "suffering" carriers slow to market will experience as IP cable telephony matures and reaches critical mass.

Industry players concur that, while current technology supports IP cable telephony services, the operational complexity of rolling services out to the subscriber base of tens of millions of households and the need to establish a profitable and sustainable business model are risk factors. Companies like AT&T Broadband and Cox are therefore conducting trials in select markets before introducing IP cable telephony to all of their subscribers.

Despite the need to solidify the business models that govern internal operations, external partnerships, and a phased introduction of new services to consumers, IP cable telephony and other digital cable services hold tremendous economic value. From an internal industry perspective, greater investments will be made to strengthen the infrastructure and to expand broadband penetration to bring full convergence to bear on the marketplace. But the economic value of convergence, particularly with regard to IP cable telephony, will only increase as subscribers are introduced to an entirely new world of communications and price barriers are no longer an obstacle.

Robin Bordoli, associate partner of Mobius Venture Capital, contends that economic value is created when closed systems are blown open. Convergence, particularly as it relates to the complete integration of telephony, cable, and media, "enables you to do the thing you are already doing better, faster, and cheaper," according to Bordoli, but it also lets you do things that you have never done before. Convergence deconstructs the entire concept of communications, whether it be person-to-person or via the media. This reality strengthens the conviction among analysts and industry executives that IP cable telephony, as well as other IP services, holds tremendous economic potential.

Convergence is poised to explode the somewhat static world of telecommunications as previously defined by the PSTN. Analysts at Gartner Consulting feel that creating a broadband-based Internet infrastructure will open the door for more aggressive innovation. David Rendall, group vice president for Gartner, articulated the firm's position this way: "We believe that the entire telco, cable, Internet and data industry will evolve into a new structure that creates a stable broadband information access environment with equal access imperatives and a dynamic services economy. This is all necessary to lead the United States into the advanced information services economy."[9]

IP cable telephony and other high-speed digital cable services hold significant value as vehicles of innovation, profit centers, and profit drivers. As the numbers in this chapter suggest, MSOs can anticipate that they will derive greater revenues from a growing subscriber base of consumer and enterprise customers, but, more important, industry participants and investors will continue to make significant investments to further develop the IP infrastructure.

## Notes

1. National Cable & Telecommunications Association (NCTA), "Cable Telephony: Offering Consumers Competitive Choice," July 2001, p. 1.
2. Ibid., p. 2.
3. Frost & Sullivan, "U.S. IP Cable Telephony Market," #6055-61, 2001, p. 1.
4. Ron Archer, "Five Movie Studios Announce Broadband Movie-On-Demand Service," pulver.com, August 17, 2001.
5. Frost & Sullivan, "US IP Cable Telephony Market," #6055-61, 2001, p. 7.
6. NCTA, "Cable Telephony: Offering Consumers Competitive Choice," July 2001, p. 5.
7. eMarketer, "The Broadband Report," April 2001, p. 16.
8. Seth Schiesel and Andrew Ross Sorkin, "Comcast Wins Bid for AT&T's Cable," *New York Times*, December 20, 2001, www.nytimes.com.
9. Dan Malossi and Travis Harrison, "Broadband Information Access Is the Key to Driving Next Generation of IT Innovation," pulver.com, December 13, 2001.

# CHAPTER EIGHT

# Lions, Tigers, and Bears:
## The Powers Behind Convergent Services

The names of some of the companies that are the most active in convergence have been mentioned throughout this book. These examples were meant to give you a quick introduction to what companies in the service and technology sectors are doing to advance convergence. This closing chapter, however, provides a much more detailed examination of the business models, metrics, and performance benchmarks being established by the industry's most powerful players in IP telephony and VoIP.

The market for convergence professionals is steadily growing, with companies expected to spend an estimated $14.86 billion for convergence services and equipment in 2004 (see Table 8-1).[1] More and more second-generation IP companies are joining VoIP pioneers to compete for these dollars.

Companies that are leaders in the move to convergence share similar business models that deal with:

1. The development of profit centers for IP telephony services

**Table 8-1. Corporate expenditures for convergence services and equipment (U.S.).**

| Expenditures (Billions) | 2000 | 2001 | 2002 | 2003 | 2004 | Growth (2002-2004) |
|---|---|---|---|---|---|---|
| | $1.95 | $5.34 | $7.81 | $10.50 | $14.86 | 47.44 percent |
| CAGR (2000-2004) | 66.1 percent | | | | | |

2. The inclusion of convergence services within this profit center

3. The design of metrics that suit the goals and operations of the company and its customers

4. The addition of strategic partnerships and acquisitions

The next section examines how each of these four strategies is being executed among the top companies in convergence.

## How They Operate: Business Models for Convergence Services

### Professional Services as a Separate Profit Center

Most companies that offer customer or professional services in IP telephony establish a separate profit center for these services, rather than incorporate the revenues earned from such activities into an overall product sales or service channel. Recording revenue earned from professional services in this arena as a specific profit center makes it easy to measure demand and growth for these particular services and thus to gauge the growth of the overall marketplace. The amount of revenue brought in by these dedicated services then becomes a benchmark for evaluating how services in IP telephony compare to the company's other service and product areas. Manufacturers set up a separate P&L center by either establishing a profit center with P&L objectives within the larger company for the group in question or actually creating a separate unit or business within the organization that provides these professional services. Nortel Global Professional Services, Siemens Advanced Customer Solutions, and Cisco's professional services department, which operates as part of the company's Customer Advocacy area, have established profit centers for professional services in IP telephony. 3Com and Alcatel have created separate businesses within their companies, allowing them to leverage their own talent and strategic partnerships just as a self-contained business would do. In the case of Nortel, Siemens, and Cisco, these subsidiary companies operate in a fashion consistent with the overall operations and relationships of the organization and have less autonomy.

Each of these manufacturers, however, uses its VoIP products to sell its services. Nortel gives its clients the option to bundle services with the product package or to purchase them individually, thus creating a customized product/service package. Cisco, on the other hand, does not offer bundled packages, making service recommendations for an additional cost. Siemens's professional services are included in the sales process, but it is the customer's decision as to whether services will be bundled with equipment or purchased separately. The same holds for Alcatel. 3Com is an interesting case in that it has parlayed its leadership as a network solutions provider and now offers professional services along with its "Voice, Video, and Data Convergence" solution.

## Convergence Services as a Subset of IP Telephony

While the endgame for IP telephony is full convergence, the marketplace is still evolving, as is the array of available convergent services. Thus, many manufacturers and service providers that maintain a separate profit center for IP telephony do not do so solely for revenues derived from convergent services and applications. These are included within the IP telephony P&L. In addition, these organizations have varying levels of resources dedicated to providing and/or developing convergent services. Avaya, for example, has a separate practice for convergence within its professional services department, as do Siemens and AT&T. Cisco offers convergent services only on demand. Alcatel, on the other hand, maintains a dedicated staff for its convergence services department, which is a subset of its professional services group. Telephony service providers are all over the map in terms of their offerings. Verizon does not maintain a separate practice for convergence services but is targeting convergence customers with its offerings. SBC offers dedicated convergence services as a part of its overall service department, which focuses on network design, network management, and call management services.

## Establishment of Metrics

Building any organization in the modern business world requires that the company establish a strong infrastructure with specific goals. But, in order to accomplish these goals, the business must maintain a certain level of flexibility. In Chapter 3, we looked at the manner in which Adir was created and was able to take advantage of a rapidly evolving technology platform and marketplace through its dedicated focus on maintaining levels of quality and profitability that could be supported only by a sound business model. The benchmarks we established in our company, whether they pertained to profitability, marketshare, technological advance, or human resource issues, helped us sustain the level of performance needed to achieve Adir's stated business goals. These benchmarks became metrics by which we assessed our performance on an ongoing basis. Metrics have proven to be critical to all of the companies leading the convergence arena as they strive to measure their success, the quality of their offerings, and their ability to consistently meet the needs of customers. The key to using metrics to accomplish all of these things is that they must be customized to fit the organization. Metrics are useful only if they are tailored to measure performance against the unique goals, business model, and internal operations of the organization. This section reviews how some of the largest equipment vendors and service providers have used their own sets of metrics to outperform their competition in the convergence arena.

Without the networking equipment provided by manufacturers, there would be no convergence services or applications; so it makes sense that, for this group customer, satisfaction is a priority. Measurables include contract extensions and percentage of repeat customers. To support these efforts, many manufacturers have initiated rigorous customer service and training programs within their organizations. In addition to customer satisfaction, companies like Alcatel, Nortel, and Cisco believe that increasing customers, ensuring quality, and minimizing operational costs together constitute a recipe for success. Methods and programs tailored to the unique aspects of each company are used to achieve these objectives. 3Com has been aggressively acquiring companies and seeking out partnerships with system integrators and distribution channels in order to provide the most comprehensive network solutions possible. Nortel employs a detailed system of surveys and feedback to ensure that customer demands are met and that each project meets its own set of success criteria. Alcatel's goals to grow faster than the market while reducing operating costs are realized through a combination of flexible service agreements designed to evolve with network technology, dedicated reviews of service agreements with customers, and a formalized process for program management and project quality. Alcatel believes that that most important metric signaling its success is the growing competitiveness of its customers. Avaya employs a similar program of customer feedback and formalized internal processes to manage costs and ensure quality.

The primary goal of systems integrators and companies that offer consulting services is to provide the most comprehensive and diverse network service possible. Revenue, market share, and customer satisfaction will follow. By providing "best-in-breed" solutions, employing staff that can handle customers' mission-critical networking needs, and instituting unforgiving internal and external feedback programs, systems integrators and consulting firms have been able to meet industry benchmarks.

Among system integrators and consultants, EDS, SAIC, AT&T Solutions, IBM's Global Services, KPMG, and Accenture seem to be leading the pack. Each company has its own metrics around which its operations and goals are organized, and each employs a variety of different methods in order to meet its own unique objectives. EDS evaluates customer satisfaction for thousands of customers on a weekly basis through an Internet tool; the results are then assessed by the company's CIO. Key success variables include repeat business and the quality of client delivery, effectiveness of the sales group, and the appropriateness of solutions offered to customers. For SAIC, the main objective is to double the revenue earned from professional services each year. To do this, SAIC uses a customer feedback process in which a project management team works closely with each customer during the course of the project. Once the project is completed, an independent customer satisfaction review is conducted on the basis of the company's standard corporate guidelines. These results are then shared with the project team and the account team. IBM Global Services focuses on partnerships. The company believes that its global reach and its access to the industry's top products supports customer growth and satisfaction. KPMG looks at revenue to determine whether or not it's meeting company objectives. For KPMG, increases in revenue are a direct result of the quality of its professional services. The firm invests heavily in employee training programs; each employee is required to take at least twenty hours of training annually.

## Partnerships

As we discussed in an earlier chapter, establishing formal partnerships has become a core aspect of the business model adopted by manufacturers and service providers. Partnering with companies that can either augment a company's product or service or complete that company's portfolio results in an increased number of customers and greater revenue at minimal cost for both partners. Manufacturers, in particular, have found partnerships to be a crucial piece of their business model, with the top six equipment makers establishing relationships with the leading service providers, system integrators, and value-added resellers (VARs).

The initial partnership model was one that companies used third parties to deliver their convergent products and services. Today, partnering companies join together to develop and deliver products and services that reflect the competencies of both partners. For manufacturers that partner with service providers and VARs, the advantages are clear: they can leverage their strengths and maximize resources, extend brand recognition, and tap into new customer bases.

The partnership models I have described are playing out in the field through a variety of specialized programs. Cisco provides its convergence services primarily through third parties via Cisco's Professional Services Partner program (PSP) and Specialized Channel Partner program (SCP). Cisco provides some services through its own Customer Advocacy

Group; however, the PSP and SCP participants provide the bulk of the company's convergence services. The PSP program companies provide planning, designing, implementation, and operational guidance for customers that use Cisco products. The SCP program has more than one hundred certified participants who represent the company's IP telephony specialists. PSP participants include Unisys, Compaq, Nextira, SAIC, IBM Global Services, NCR, and KPMG. SBC and EDS are SCPs.

Nortel has chosen to limit its partnership program to just a few companies, opting to use internal service departments to provide convergence services. Nortel's Internal Global Professional Services group provides customers with enterprise networking, call centers, and ISP solutions. The company has also developed a Premier Service Provider (PSP) program to support partners that sell Nortel solutions. Nortel's primary partners are Hewlett Packard, which works with Nortel's PSP group; Accenture, which provides systems integration services; and IBM, which uses Nortel solutions as part of its ecommerce offerings.

3Com has established a Convergence Leadership Alliance Program that is used in conjunction with internal service professionals to assist convergence customers. The alliance program offers partners systems integration training and collaboration, end user solution consultation, and assistance with the design, deployment, and support of convergence solutions. 3Com has also established an internal consulting services group to assist its direct sales channels and partner sales channels in these areas. The four practices within 3Com's consulting group are multimedia convergence, customer contact centers, enterprise mobility, and ecommerce.

Unlike the companies just mentioned, Alcatel is almost completely dependent on third-party partners that provide convergence services to the company's enterprise customers. Alcatel's primary partners are Norstan, which offers maintenance solutions, and SAIC, which acts as a systems integrator for Alcatel customers. Adir has created several different types of partnership programs in order to address all of the challenges inherent in the telecommunications marketplace. Strategic partners work with us to develop new technologies and create business models that foster the commercialization of these innovations. Adir uses technology partners to explore interoperable VoIP solutions. In this program we partner with Cisco, Motorola, digiquant, Mind CTI, and Portal Software. Adir's system integrators use Adir solutions in their offering and help customers integrate and optimize our company's products. Our system integration partners are Getronics, Netsmart, SYSCOM, and Datacraft. Our last partnership program involves other network carriers (which in turn supply service providers with services and solutions); these are our call termination partners. Our call termination partners offer service providers special rates, customized packages, and expedited deployment of certain applications.

## How the Leaders Stack Up

With turbulence in the market and company valuations in flux, an appropriate way to determine market leaders is to consider a combination of financial measures and corporate competencies—technical strengths, achievements in customer retention and distribution, and revenue growth strategies.

What we have seen in recent years in the industry is a shift of market dominance from the bellwethers like Cisco, Nortel, and 3Com to under-the-radar companies such as Avaya. In both the technology and the service sectors, companies that have been operating for a few years are now really coming into their own to challenge the industry Goliaths. Part of the reason for this is that these companies entered the marketplace cautiously, carefully seeking out long-term customers and distribution opportunities. They didn't get caught up in the tech frenzy or rely solely on dot-coms to purchase their equipment or services. Cisco is an example of a telecom that experienced tremendous growth precisely because it was selling equipment to Internet-based companies during the headiest days of the Internet boom. Avaya took a different path to growth, targeting large enterprise customers for its equipment and software. While it couldn't avoid a downturn in revenue, it did experience strong sales in 2001, and its net income loss was held to less than one billion dollars. The same cannot be said for its primary competitors, Cisco and Nortel. This section examines the convergence leaders among manufacturers, consultants, and telephony service providers and gives you some insight into the competencies that will drive the IP telephony business for the long term.

There are many players, both large and small, in the telecommunications manufacturing space, but only a few dominate this arena in terms of their technical strengths. The obvious leaders include Nortel, Siemens, Cisco, 3Com, and Alcatel. There are a few that are lesser known but that have emerged as strong players in both market share and technological innovation. The most successful of these is Avaya. Industry analysts consider Avaya a leader in the area of convergence technology, with strong competencies in planning and design; integration, implementation, and operations; and applications. Of the bellwether companies, Alcatel, Nortel, and Siemens have the best capabilities in these areas. Cisco comes in a close second, with limited functionality in planning and design. Interestingly, companies like Juniper and Lucent, which previously dominated the telecom space, have not emerged as leaders in convergence.

## Avaya

Formerly the enterprise networking arm of Lucent, Avaya was spun off to Lucent shareholders in 2000 and since then has dominated the enterprise networking market for IP telephony. Its customers include more than 90 percent of Fortune 500 companies, as well as government agencies. Avaya's equipment and software solutions provide corporate customers with interactive voice response, email, and Web access. In addition to manufacturing this equipment, Avaya provides consulting services and outsourcing solutions. Understanding early on that cable will play a crucial role in driving convergence, Avaya also manufactures network cabling products.

Avaya is a global organization with in-depth knowledge and expertise in both telecommunications technology and service. As a Lucent spinoff, Avaya has a staff that is made up largely of former Lucent employees, and the company boasts an experienced knowledge base. Industry analysts gave Avaya the highest ratings in all areas of convergence competencies. The organization has a solid business model that allows it to offer a diverse portfolio of products and services to customers worldwide.

In addition to manufacturing convergence equipment, Avaya offers professional services to customers who either own their own equipment or who outsource both the equipment and services from Avaya. The primary service area for Avaya is call center management. Avaya provides engineering, design, and outsourcing services in this area. Avaya also provides professional service in two applications areas: customer relationship management (CRM) and unified communication. In both of these areas, Avaya supplies consulting, integration management, and support solutions.

Avaya's strategic model includes partnership and outsourcing programs; however, the bulk of Avaya's technology solutions and professional services are supported by Avaya Labs and its services group. Avaya Labs focus on five research areas:

- Converged communications and IP telephony

- Speech and multimedia technologies

- Data analysis designed to advance applications in CRM and data mining

- Quality of service

- Security, ranging from authentication to ensuring the security of endpoints and applications in the network

Eleven thousand of Avaya's more than twenty thousand employees are service professionals who support a worldwide clientele by planning, designing, implementing, and managing converged voice and data networks, CRM systems, and unified messaging solutions. Avaya has a tremendous global presence, operating in approximately fifty-one countries. This visibility increased when Avaya provided the network connections for the 2002 FIFA World Cup. To do this, Avaya had to build and manage perhaps one of the world's largest and most complex converged networks that connected twenty stadiums in Japan and Korea, more than forty thousand volunteer and press centers, ten thousand media broadcast centers, and the FIFA committee in Japan and Korea. All together, Avaya networks had to connect between four thousand and five thousand communication and data devices, as well of hundreds of network switches and routers.

How do Avaya's enterprise solutions play out in the real world? As discussed in Chapter 6, converged communications greatly increases productivity for large enterprises, particularly those with international offices. Through voice mail servers, unified messaging, and visual desktop messaging, companies are connected in real time throughout the entire organization, whether the employees are in the home office, at a satellite location, or on the road. Avaya's CRM solutions have been used by a broad range of customers, from transportation organizations to health care and insurance providers. These solutions integrate front- and back-office demands, provision Internet call centers, and support sales growth through Internet text chat applications.

Financial service companies use Avaya's solutions to expand customer relationships, deliver multichannel access, and securely network a virtual enterprise that must operate in real time with mission-critical information and applications. Retailers and manufacturers benefit from Avaya's CRM solutions and those applications that help optimize their supply chain. Health care companies can reliably network high volumes of critical calls and sensitive information, enabling mobile medical staff with accurate information quickly and reliably. Service providers make use of Avaya's solutions to differentiate their own services without having to invest in building new systems from the ground up.

## 3Com

Founded in 1979, 3Com employs approximately three thousand engineers at its U.S. locations. The company offers a broad range of services to its enterprise customers, including network design, configuration, installation, and management, as well as project management. Convergence services are just one aspect of what the company provides its clients. 3Com's convergence customers are small to medium-size companies looking for help in convergence/VoIP readiness, multimedia convergence, or call center management. To support its convergence services, 3Com has established a leadership alliance program designed to deliver integrated packages of network support and services for convergence. Key participants include Siemens, Hewlett Packard, IBM Global Services, Accenture, and KPMG (see Table 8-2).

In comparative studies, 3Com did not rank as strongly overall as competitors like Avaya and Cisco, primarily because it lacks competency in applications management for convergence services and because certain aspects of its technology (e.g., bandwidth management, network security) were not as highly regarded as those of its competitors. However,

**Table 8-2. Key partnerships among convergence leaders.**

| Manufacturers | Cisco | Nortel | 3Com | Alcatel | Siemens |
|---|---|---|---|---|---|
| VARs | Norstan | Compaq | Norstan | Norstan | Norstan |
| | Compaq | Unisys | HP | | |
| | Unisys | HP | | | |
| | Nextira | Nextira | | | |
| | NCR | NCR | | | |
| | Adir Technologies | | | | |
| Consultants & Systems Integrators | KPMG | PWC | PWC | IBM | |
| | IBM Global Services | Accenture | KPMG | SAIC | |
| | EDS | IBM | Accenture | | |
| | SAIC | EDS | IBM | | |
| | | SAIC | SAIC | | |
| Network Service Providers | SBC | | | Verizon | |
| | BellSouth | | | | |

3Com does get strong marks in providing real-world convergence opportunities to its customers. These applications include customer contact centers, enterprise mobility, multimedia convergence, and ebusiness solutions. It is also adept in creating the alliances and partnerships needed to support the changing and increasingly demanding needs of enterprise customers. Unlike some of its competitors, 3Com brings its channel partners and system integrators into the consulting process early in determining a customer's needs and specific capabilities. This, in combination with its Leadership Alliance Program and the ongoing work of the 3Com Lab, enables 3Com to be among the best companies providing end-to-end convergence solutions to its customers.

3Com's 2001 financial results were not stellar. With $2.8 billion in sales in 2001, the company experienced a 53 percent drop from the previous year. Revenue in 2002 was hit even harder. The company booked $1.5 billion, resulting in a negative sales growth of 47.6 percent from 2001 to 2002. Net income results were slightly more positive. Net income for 2001 was a negative $965 million, while in 2002 it was a negative $596 billion. Perhaps this is a result of restructuring and consolidation in 2002 that reorganized the company into two business units, a Business Networks Company (BNC), its LAN network equipment arm, and CommWorks, its carrier network business, focusing on IP networking and telephony.

## Cisco

Cisco is arguably a household name (heck, it was even featured in a TV episode of *The Simpsons*). The company is forever linked with the concept of open communication and the phenomenon of the Internet. While Cisco's rise and sustained profitability have become the stuff of Internet legend, in recent times Cisco has had to reposition itself in order to hold onto its once lofty status. To do this, the company has embraced convergence and VoIP, partnering with other equipment manufacturers, network providers, and carriers. This strategy has helped the company rebound from a saturation of its core products (i.e., routers) and has created new customers to replace the dot.coms that have closed. Cisco's ability to identify emerging markets and to create the equipment to serve those markets, as well as its ability to partner with industry leaders, is largely responsible for the company's ability to innovate and to expand its product portfolio and customer base.

Cisco is among the most powerful equipment makers in the IP telephony arena, with nearly half of the service providers in this sector using Cisco gateways. Balancing its market dominance is the unfailing business acumen of Cisco's senior leadership. Despite slight losses in profitability throughout 2001 and 2002, Cisco has been able to maintain a high market cap and has reserved enough capital to sustain its operational performance, as well as to fund ventures into new technology arenas. The company did have to reexamine its tertiary alliances and affiliations in an effort to redirect resources, and unfortunately it did suffer layoffs. The IP telephony market represents a strong piece of Cisco's future, a sentiment vocalized by the company's chairman and CEO, John Chambers, on numerous occasions in 2001 and 2002. Through partnerships with other equipment makers, as well as ISPs and VoIP service providers, Cisco has created new demand for its hardware and Internet solutions. Analysts commend the company for its ability to create such alliances and to expand into a number of markets simultaneously. However, perhaps the range of products that Cisco offers also represents a weakness for the company. Analysts and observers have noted that the company struggles to deliver the level of customer support desired by the marketplace, particularly for packet telephony products. In addition, the breadth of Cisco's product portfolio compared to that of some of its smaller competitors deflects the company's attention from its efforts to develop equipment, services, and solutions in IP telephony.

That being said, Cisco is among the strongest financial performers of recent fiscal years. At the close of the 2001 fiscal year, the company had earned $18.9 billion in sales, representing a slight decline in sales growth. The company's net income was in the black as well, at $1.9 billion—an achievement when compared to results at many of its competitors, whose net income was in the negative. See Table 8-3 for further comparison.

## Companies to Watch

### Alcatel

One of France's leading industrial companies, Alcatel traces its history back to 1898, when it began as Compagnie Générale d'Electricité (CGE), in competition with Siemens and General Electric at the time. Despite its decidedly low-tech beginnings, Alcatel has become one of the best-known and most powerful companies in IP telephony worldwide. The company employs a global workforce of ninety-nine thousand in 130 countries, providing service to medium and large businesses that use IP networks. Alcatel is a one-stop shop for businesses that use VoIP and other convergent technologies. It diagnoses communications networks; consults on the choice of architecture and budgetary considerations; plans, designs, and integrates systems; troubleshoots and manages systems once they are in place; and offers project management help. Of the crop of service providers that offer convergent solutions, Alcatel is among the most credentialed, with

**Table 8-3. Financial comparison of leading convergence companies.**

| | 3Com | Avaya | Alcatel | Cisco | Deltathree | IBasis | ITXC | Nortel | Lucent | Juniper |
|---|---|---|---|---|---|---|---|---|---|---|
| **2001 Sales (Billions)** | 2.8 | 6.8 | 22.6 | 22.3 | .016 | .134 | .173 | 17.5 | 21.3 | .887 |
| **1-Year Sales Growth** | (53.5 percent) | (11.5 percent) | (23.6 percent) | 17.8 percent | (48.4 percent) | 118.6 percent | 104.2 percent | (42.2 percent) | (37 percent) | 31.7 percent |
| **2001 Net Income (Billions)** | (.965) | (.352) | (4.4) | (1.01) | (035.7) | (.191) | (.176) | (27.3) | (16.2) | (.134) |
| **2001 Employees** | 8,165 | 23,000 | 99,000 | 38,000 | 152 | 441 | 224 | 53,600 | 77,000 | 1,227 |
| **2001 Revenue per Employee** | $342,927 | $295,652 | $228,283 | $586,842 | | | | $326,493 | $276,623 | $722,901 |
| **2001 Employee Growth** | (25.5 percent) | (25.8 percent) | (24.8 percent) | 11.8 percent | (30.9 percent) | 31.6 percent | (26.1 percent) | (43.3 percent) | (38.9 percent) | 32.4 percent |

decades of experience developing network applications and tools. The company also delivers "end-to-end" Internet solutions over its own network.

Alcatel's financial performance in 2001 was consistent with that of its competitors: in the black for net sales ($22.6 billion, representing a decrease of 23.6 percent) and in the red for net income, at a negative $4.4 billion.

## Genuity

Described as a venerable Internet pioneer, Genuity provides enterprise IP network services and manages converged Internet services. Genuity customers range from network developers like Sun Microsystems to Web companies such as Yahoo! and AOL. The company has struggled during the past several years with the industrywide turn in the tech marketplace and will be acquired by Level 3 in a deal valued at $242 million. In 2001, Genuity brought in net sales of $1.2 billion, up 7.4 percent from the previous year, but its net income plummeted by almost $4 billion.

Genuity is viewed as a valuable acquisition because of the quality of its VoIP network. Created to eliminate any single point of failure for network and infrastructure elements, including power, network connectivity, transport, and equipment, Genuity's fiber backbone spans 17,500 miles in the United States alone and has global reach.

## ITXC (Internet Telephony Exchange Carrier)

ITXC is a wholesale IP telephony carrier, meaning that it provides ISPs, phone carriers, and Web portals with a way to make calls over its own proprietary IP network. Founded in July 1997, and managed for many years by Tom Euslin, the company offered its first commercial products nine months later, in April 1998. Analysts have commended the Company for driving innovations in convergence solutions, particularly in PC-to-phone and ecommerce.

ITXC has been able to leverage VoIP's cost-saving advantages and simultaneously increase its traffic volume and revenue for several reasons:

■ Its customer base consists of both traditional and next-generation retail service providers, including the top U.S-based international carriers, RBOCs, and international carriers such as China Telecom, Telstra, Cable and Wireless, and Optus, for which ITXC terminates traffic to multiple international destinations. With such a wide customer base, ITXC is less likely to be affected by changes in investor and market preferences in any one region of the world.

■ Partnerships with incumbent and emerging telecommunications carriers in various countries increases the number of countries and termination routes ITXC can offer to its customers, diversifies its customer portfolio, and helps the company quickly gain economies of scale.

■ ITXC has entered relatively untapped, recently deregulated markets, such as Zimbabwe, Bolivia, and Chile, in addition to countries in the Middle East and the Asian Pacific. Increased traffic in less competitive markets has generated higher-margin revenues.

■ ITXC acts as an enabler of competition in recently liberalized markets by encouraging the adoption of IP networks to improve the existing telecommunications infrastructure instead of expanding circuit-switched networks.

ITXC's financial performance in 2001 was much better than those of its competitors as a whole. Net sales increased by an incredible 104.2 percent, reaching $173.2 million. Like that of its competitors, ITXC's net income declined, to a negative $176.4 million in 2001.

## Note

1. InfoTech, "Professional Services for Converged Networks and Applications: A Competitive Analysis of Leading Providers," June 2001, p. 20.

# Epilogue

The call has been heard around the world: IP convergence will change our personal and business lives directly. The wide breadth of companies and service providers in convergence are now coalescing around standards and technologies that will become increasingly more prevalent.

The challenge will be to deliver scalable convergence solutions that are clear winners. These are solutions that once in place will be difficult to give up. We now stand at the cusp of this event and outstanding opportunity.

We can all be winners in convergence by helping to understand it better, and to guide its implementation as it unfolds. We hope that our experience and this book has helped.

# Glossary*

All company names, products, and services mentioned are the trademarks or registered trademarks of their respective owners.

## A

**American National Standards Institute (ANSI)**
An organization that develops and publishes voluntary standards for a wide range of industries based in the United States.

**America's Carriers Telecommunications Association (ACTA)**
A coalition of small long-distance carriers. Based in Casselberry, FL, the group was founded in 1985 by fifteen small long-distance companies to "provide national representation before legislative and regulatory bodies, while continuing to improve industry business relations." There are now more than 165 members.

**Application Service Provider (ASP)**
A company that provides remote access to applications, usually over the Internet. ASPs are used when an organization

*Reprinted with the permission of Intel Corporation.

finds it more cost-effective to have someone else host its applications than to install, implement, and maintain the applications at its own facility. The applications can be as simple as access to a remote file server or as complex as an enterprise management system accessed through a standard browser. Most ASPs provide the servers, network access, and applications for a monthly or yearly subscription fee.

**Asynchronous Transfer Mode (ATM)**
A 53-byte cell-switching technology well suited for carrying voice, data, and video traffic on the same infrastructure. It is inherently scalable in throughput and was designed to provide quality of service (QoS).

**Automatic Call Distributor (ACD)**
A specialized phone system that handles incoming calls or makes outgoing calls. Commonly used in call centers, an ACD can recognize and answer an incoming call, look in its database for instructions on what to do with that call, play a recorded message for the caller (using instructions from the database), and send the caller to a live operator as soon as the operator is free or as soon as the caller has listened to the recorded message.

# B

**Broadband**
High-speed voice, data, and video networked services that are digital, interactive, and packet based. The bandwidth is 384 Kbps or higher, and 384 Kbps is widely accepted as the minimum bandwidth required to enable full-frame-rate digital video.

# C

**Competitive Local Exchange Carrier (CLEC)**
Created by the Telecommunications Act of 1996, a CLEC is a service provider that is in direct competition with an incum-

bent service provider. "CLEC" is often used as a general term for any competitor, but the term actually has legal implications. To become a CLEC, a service provider must be granted "CLEC status" by a state's Public Utilities Commission. In exchange for the time and money spent to gain CLEC status, the CLEC is entitled to co-locate its equipment in the incumbent's central office, which saves the CLEC considerable expense.

**Computer Telephony (CT)**
The addition of computer intelligence to the making, receiving, and managing of telephone calls.

**CT Server**
A standards-based open telephony server for delivering services in a business enterprise or telephone central office. At its core is software that allows multiple applications and technologies from different vendors to interoperate on one server.

**Customer Interaction Management (CIM)**
The technology and processes associated with handling multiple customer communications touch points, including telephony, email, and Web-site interaction.

**Customer Relationship Management (CRM)**
The way in which a company manages interactions with its customers. A successful CRM solution depends on an ability to interact with customers through any channel they choose, as well as a way to track and maintain real-time records of customer interactions so that a complete view of the customer is always available.

# D

**Dialed Number Identification Service (DNIS)**
A telephone service that identifies the number that the caller dialed for the receiver of the call. DNIS is a common feature

of 800 and 900 services and can identify the number originally dialed when multiple 800 or 900 numbers terminate on the same destination trunks. DNIS works by passing the dialed number to the destination device, which can act upon this data to control its routing, queuing, IVR, or other call behavior. DNIS is typically used to separate call treatment for different inbound campaigns or help desk numbers, whether in one enterprise or at a service bureau. Caller ID systems are based on the DNIS.

### Digital Signal Processor (DSP)
A specialized digital microprocessor that performs calculations on digitized signals that were originally analog and then forwards the results. The big advantage of DSPs lies in their programmability. DSPs can be used to compress voice signals to as little as 4,800 bps. DSPs are an integral part of all voice processing systems and fax machines.

### Digital Subscriber Line (DSL)
A technology that allows a provider to use the excess bandwidth found in a copper line for the provision of data services. While this technology was meant to make use of an enormous copper infrastructure until fiber optic cable was fully deployed, it has become an industry unto itself. xDSL is used to describe all of the "flavors" of DSL in general.

### Double Data Rate (DDR)
A term used to describe a synchronous DRAM (see SDRAM), which transfers data on both edges of the system clock (rather than just one edge), thus doubling the data transfer rate.

### Dual-Tone Multifrequency (DTMF)
A way of signaling consisting of a push-button or touchtone dial that sends out a sound consisting of two discrete tones that are picked up and interpreted by telephone switches (either PBXs or central offices).

**Dynamic Synchronous Transfer Mode (DTM)**
A dynamic circuit switch technology that provides transport between routers through channels and enables high-speed optical transport. In DTM, a channel has a dedicated band-width and forms a dynamic route between the sender and receiver, passing through the routers along the path. Quality-of-service (QoS) channels are established on the fly and set up extremely quickly. Routers along a channel's path easily pass data from one link to the next, as no address informa-tion must be checked. No packets need to be stored in buff-ers, so no packet buffers are needed. Consequently, there is no risk of the buffer overflow, which could lead to packet loss and net congestion.

# E

**Edge Switch**
A network-switching device designed to perform functions usually associated with a router in a LAN or WAN environ-ment.

**Enterprise Computer Telephony Forum (ECTF)**
A nonprofit, California-based organization that develops computer telephony standards.

**eXtensible Markup Language (xML)**
A coding system that allows any type of information to be delivered across the World Wide Web in a structured man-ner. As a meta-language, it contains rules for constructing other markup languages and allows the creation of tags that expand the type and quantity of information that can be pro-vided about data held in documents. It shares with HTML the common heritage of the SGML (Standard Generalized Markup Language) standard. However, unlike HTML, xML is truly general purpose. The World Wide Web Consortium

completed xML in early 1998, and the standard has quickly gained industrywide, multivendor acceptance.

## F

**Federal Communications Commission (FCC)**
The U.S. federal agency responsible for regulating interstate and international communications by radio, television, wire, satellite, and cable.

## G

**Gatekeeper**
A component of the ITU H.323 "umbrella" of standards defining real-time multimedia communications and conferencing for packet-based networks. The gatekeeper is the central control entity that performs management functions in a voice and fax over IP networks and for multimedia applications such as video conferencing. Gatekeepers provide intelligence for the network, including address resolution, authorization, and authentication services, the logging of call detail records, and communications with network management systems. Gatekeepers also monitor the network for engineering purposes, as well as for real-time network management and load balancing, control bandwidth, and provide interfaces to existing legacy systems.

**Gateway**
An entrance into and out of a communications network. Technically, a gateway is an electronic repeater device that intercepts and steers electrical signals from one network to another.

**G.lite**
A version of ADSL (see DSL) that delivers 1.5 Mbps downstream and 640 kbps upstream and is specifically tailored for

the consumer market segment. G.lite reduces the need for phone companies to send out a representative to complete an onsite installation by decreasing the need for new wiring and for a special signal "splitter" that separates voice and data at the user's home. G.lite delivers "always-on" Internet access at high speeds using existing wiring and allowing the concurrent use of normal telephone service.

# H

### H.110

A physical-layer computer telephony or TDM bus specification, used for connecting board-level resources within a CompactPCI chassis. For example, an H.110 bus is used to bridge channels between a T-1/E-1 interface board and a DSP resource board. The H.110 bus supports up to 4,096 simultaneous channels. Within a CPCI system, the H.110 bus is physically implemented within a fixed mid-plane, greatly facilitating board removal and hot-swap when compared with older style ribbon-cable overlays.

### H.323

An ITU-T standard for packet-based multimedia communications systems. This standard defines the different multimedia entities that make up a multimedia system— Endpoint, Gateway, Multipoint Conferencing Unit (MCU), and Gatekeeper—and their interaction. This standard is used for many voice-over IP applications and is heavily dependent on other standards, mainly H.225 and H.245.

# I

### Incumbent Local Exchange Carrier (ILEC)

Typically, the carrier that was granted the right to provide service as a result of the breakup of AT&T. These providers are also referred to as RBOCs (Regional Bell Operating Companies) or Baby Bells.

### Integrated Access Device (IAD)

A customer premise device that processes voice and LAN traffic for a single local connection to the wide-area network.

### Integrated Communications Provider (ICP)

A communications carrier that provides both network facilities and tailored packages for businesses, including voice, data, and secure applications. These services are provided simultaneously through the same channel (such as a POTS, DSL, or cable line). Through an ICP, users are able to secure all their communications services from one provider and receive one all-inclusive bill.

### Integrated Services Digital Network (ISDN)

A new network designed to improve the world's telecommunications services by providing an internationally accepted standard for voice, data, and signaling; by making all transmission circuits end-to-end digital; by adopting a standard out-of-band signaling system; and by bringing more bandwidth to the desktop.

### Interactive Voice Response (IVR)

Links callers with information in databases. This technology allows callers to complete transactions or queries over the phone. Automatic Speech Recognition (ASR) is fast replacing the DTMF method of activating IVR services and is one of the most important recent innovations in telephony-based self-service.

### International Telecommunications Union (ITU)

An organization established by the United Nations to set telecommunications standards, allocate frequencies to various uses, and sponsor trade shows every four years.

**Internet Engineering Task Force (IETF)**
One of two technical working bodies in the Internet Activities Board. It meets three times a year to set the technical standards for the Internet.

**Internet Messaging Application Protocol (IMAP)**
An Internet protocol that allows a central server to provide remote access to email messages.

**Internet Protocol (IP)**
A unique, 32-bit number for a specific TCP/IP host on the Internet, normally printed in decimal form (for example, 128.122.40.227). Part of the TCP/IP family of protocols, it describes software that tracks the Internet address of nodes, routes outgoing messages, and recognizes incoming messages.

**Internet Service Provider (ISP)**
A vendor that provides direct access to the Internet.

**IP Gatekeeper**
An H.323 entity that defines the policies that govern a multimedia system (e.g., dialing plans, user privileges, bandwidth consumption). The gatekeeper also provides the means to extract information from such a system for various purposes (e.g., billing information, users that are logged in). The gatekeeper is also a focal point for the introduction of supplementary services.

**IP Gateway**
Most commonly, a network device that converts voice and fax calls, in real time, between the public switched telephone network (PSTN) and an IP network. Primary IP gateway functions include voice, fax, compression/decompression, packetization, call routing, and control signaling. Additional features may include interfaces to external controllers, such

as gatekeepers or soft-switches, billing systems, and network management systems.

**IP PBX**
An enterprise-based IP data network device that switches VoIP telephone traffic.

**IP Telephony**
Technology that allows voice phone calls to be made over the Internet or other packet networks using a PC via gateways and standard telephones.

# L

**Lifeline POTS**
A voice telephone line that works even if electricity is cut off at the customer premises, since the line is powered from emergency backup at the central office. Multiple lifeline POTS lines can be delivered on one copper pair with the use of a digital line powered pair gain system.

**Local Exchange Carrier (LEC)**
A company that provides local telephone service.

# M

**Media Gateway**
A generic class of products grouped under the Media Gateway Control Protocol (MGCP). A major function of the media gateway is simple IP/TDM conversion under the control of a softswitch. Media gateways include, but are not limited to, the following types of equipment: stand-alone, server-based gateways, RAS-based gateways, gateway switches, traditional CO switches, and ATM switches.

**Media Server**
A device that processes multimedia applications such as call distribution, fax-on-demand, and automated email response programs. Media servers consolidate separate communications devices, often resulting in reduced startup costs, simplified maintenance and administration, and increased application development flexibility.

**Multi-Service Access Switch**
The first point of user access and exit for processing and managing traffic over high-speed broadband networks.

**Multi-Service Router**
A type of router that examines calls in the PSTN before they are sent to a particular site. A special signaling link, which can send advance notification of incoming calls, can be obtained from the central office. A pre-call routing system can receive this information, look at the current state of all call centers, and then send a notification back to the PSTN indicating where the call is to go. Thus the call is routed before it is even picked up. Post-call routing is used in cases where the decision to redirect a call is not (or cannot be) made until some time after the call is connected at a particular location.

# P

**Policy Manager**
An IP network element that enforces bandwidth assignment rules for classes of service and quality of service (QoS), as dictated by a user or a service provider.

**Presence**
The measure and status of a user's ability to communicate and be communicated with at any given moment. It includes the reception media (voice, video, instant messaging), the

user's availability, and the user's willingness to communicate by various means and through various people (even if a phone is busy, for example). It also takes into account the capabilities and characteristics of each medium (whether a phone is for business or personal use or which cell site a cell phone is in at that moment). Presence information can be distributed to interested parties through a presence service when it changes. Some specific types of presence services are "buddy lists" and "instant messengers."

### Private Branch Exchange (PBX)

A telephone switch owned privately, usually by a large company. If it owns a PBX, a company does not need to lease a telephone line for each telephone set at a site.

## R

### Real-Time Transport Protocol (RTP)

The Internet-standard protocol for the transport of real-time data, including audio and video. RTP is used in virtually all voice-over-IP architectures, for videoconferencing, media-on-demand, and other applications. A thin protocol, it supports content identification, timing reconstruction, and detection of lost packets.

## S

### SCbus

A standard bus for computer telephony hardware components. Its hybrid architecture consists of a serial message bus for control and signaling and a 16-wire TDM data bus.

### Session Initiation Protocol (SIP)

An Internet standard specified by the Internet Engineering Task Force (IETF) in RFC 2543. SIP is used to initiate, manage, and terminate interactive sessions between one or more users on the Internet. SIP, which borrows heavily from HTTP and the email protocol SMTP, provides scalability, extensibility, flexibility, and capabilities for creating new services. SIP is increasingly used for Internet telephony signaling, in gateways, PC phones, softswitches, and softphones; but it is not limited to Internet telephony and can be used to initiate and manage any type of session, including video, interactive games, and text chat.

**Skills-Based Routing**
Routing technique that takes into account individual agents' abilities, as well as their skill levels, when making real-time routing decisions. Blended agent-pool support ensures that maximum agent capacity is used during periods of peak call volume.

**Skills-Based Scheduling**
Scheduling technique that takes into account individual agents' abilities, as well as their skill levels, when forecasting and scheduling manpower needs. It accommodates agents with multiple skills. Skills scheduling allocates a number of hours per skill per agent on the basis of forecasted call center needs for that agent's particular skills. Abilities with different multimedia responses, including voice, fax, online chat, and email, are also taken into account.

**Softswitch**
Generic term for any open application program interface (API) software used to bridge a public switched telephone network and voice over Internet protocol by separating the call control functions of a phone call from the media gateway (transport layer).

**Software PBX**
A telephone system that converges voice and data on an industry-standard computing platform and uses computer te-

lephony components that conform to industry standards. Because they conform to industry standards, software PBXs are interoperable with third-party systems and CT components. Conformance also allows software PBXs to run third-party enhanced applications such as desktop call control, graphical voice mail, automatic call distribution (ACD), IP gateways, follow-me call forwarding, unified messaging, and CRM integration.

**Symmetrical Digital Subscriber Line (SDSL)**
A line in which upstream (customer premise to the network) speed is the same as downstream (network to the customer premise) speed. SDSL is found almost exclusively in business environments because, typically, residential customers do not need high upstream speed.

## T

**T-1**
Trunk Level 1. A high-speed (1.544 megabits per second) digital telephone line with the equivalent of twenty-four individual 64Kbps channels, which are joined via time division multiplexing. A T-1 can be used to transmit voice or data, and many are used to provide connections to the Internet. Also known as a DS1 or Digital Signal 1.

**TASP**
A telephony application service provider supplies companies with new telephony applications, technologies, and an infrastructure at little to no premise-based capital cost. A TASP hosts managed services and application solutions through the use of virtual private networks (VPNs), which customers can log into, and through open standard application development platforms such as XML and VoiceXML, which can

integrate almost seamlessly with the Internet. The TASP delivery model enables rapid implementation, decreases cost of ownership, and reduces the need for on-site technical expertise.

**Telephony Application Programming Interface (TAPI)**
Enables developers to write PC applications that take advantage of services provided by telephony vendors. Applications can be developed to work with telephone systems ranging from a simple Plain Old Telephone Service (POTS) connection to advanced PBXs. TAPI, for example, can enable an application to dial a telephone number, store commonly dialed numbers, record greetings, and even take dictation using speech recognition.

**Traffic Shaping**
The process by which IP flows are classified, queued, and delivered to a network to conform to the contracted service, in order to improve efficiency and minimize packet loss for traffic classified as time-sensitive or high priority.

# U

**Unified Messaging**
An application that provides a single network-based access point from which users can manage all information and message types, using any number and variety of access devices (e.g., PC, Web browser, phone), from anywhere and regardless of connection path (LAN, Internet, telephone). Unified messaging solutions seamlessly integrate voice mail, email, and fax in a single email inbox on one server. From a central digital store, all of these message types are accessible via multiple devices and interfaces with a consistent set of features and capabilities.

## V

**Voice Browser**

Similar in functionality to PC-based Web browsers, a voice browser is designed to standardize the user interface and experience for consumers browsing voice-driven content and services on the Voice Web. In contrast to a "traditional" Web browser, which resides as a client on a user's PC, a voice browser operates in a centralized server, which houses the voice resources to speak out or listen for VoiceXML-tagged content. The user's phone, in this context, is analogous to a keyboard and mouse in relation to a browser and is used to transfer user responses.

**Voice Over Internet Protocol (VoIP)**

Technology used to transmit voice conversations over a data network using the Internet Protocol. VoIP primarily builds on and complements existing standards, such as H.323.

**Voice Portal**

Services that offer access to a range of information sources from one 800 number dialed from any type of phone. Typical information includes stock market data, weather, news, sports, business locators, and audio feeds of headline news and traffic reports.

**Voice Web**

An audible "network of networks" that links the telephone network with the World Wide Web and allows Internet content and commerce to be accessed from any phone, anywhere in the world, using spoken commands.

**VoiceXML**

An emerging standard markup language that defines a common format for allowing access to Web content via the phone. VoiceXML uses XML tags to represent call flows and dialog and enables phone access, navigation, and content delivery from any Web site adhering to the standard. It also allows Web content to be delivered to wireless phone users, greatly expanding the audience for such services.

# W

**Wide Area Network (WAN)**
A communications network used to connect computers and other devices across a large area. The connection can be private or public.

**Wireless Application Protocol (WAP)**
A protocol that enables wireless phones and other wireless devices to access data over the Internet and/or Intranets and to display those data on WAP-enabled devices. WAP is an open standard and is air-link independent, which means that it works across a wide range of devices, and a broad base of manufacturers and developers is creating products for it. WAP operates on the client server model and requires software on the handset and a WAP gateway/server on the network level.

# Abbreviations and Acronyms

| | |
|---|---|
| **ACD** | Automatic Call Distributor |
| **ACTA** | America's Carriers Telecommunications Association |
| **ANSI** | American National Standards Institute |
| **ASP** | Application Service Provider |
| **ATM** | Asynchronous Transfer Mode |
| **BCP** | Broadband Communications Provider |
| **CIM** | Customer Interaction Management |
| **CLEC** | Competitive Local Exchange Carrier |
| **CPCI** | CompactPCI |
| **CRM** | Customer Relationship Management |
| **CRS** | Channelized Reserved Services |
| **CT** | Computer Telephony |
| **DDR** | Double Data Rate |
| **DNIS** | Dialed Number Identification Service |
| **DSL** | Digital Subscriber Line |
| **DSP** | Digital Signal Processor |
| **DTM** | Dynamic Synchronous Transfer Mode |

**DTMF**     Dual-Tone Multifrequency

**ECTF**     Enterprise Computer Telephony Forum

**FCC**      Federal Communications Commission

**IAD**       Integrated Access Device
**ICP**       Integrated Communications Provider
**IETF**      Internet Engineering Task Force
**IFRF**     Internet Fax Routing Forum
**ILEC**     Incumbent Local Exchange Carrier
**IMAP**    Internet Messaging Application Protocol
**IP**         Internet Protocol
**ISP**       Internet Service Provider
**ITU**       International Telecommunications Union
**IVR**       Interactive Voice Response
**IXC**       InterExchange Carrier

**LEC**      Local Exchange Carrier

**PBX**      Private Branch Exchange

**RTP**      Real-time Transport Protocol

**SDRAM**   Synchronous Dynamic Random Access Memory
**SDSL**     Symmetrical Digital Subscribe Line
**SIP**       Session Initiation Protocol

**VoIP**      Voice Over Internet Protocol

**WAN**     Wide Area Network
**WAP**     Wireless Application Protocol

**XML**      eXtensible Markup Language

# Bibliography

Auletta, Ken. *The Highwaymen.* New York: Random House, 1997.

Doyle, Lee. *Boom and Bust in Broadband Networks,* #23909. Framingham, MA: IDC, January 2001.

EMarketer. *The Broadband Report.* April 2001.

Farrand, Elizabeth. *Look Who's Talking: Web Talk User Survey, 2001.* Framingham, MA: IDC, 2001.

Farrand, Elizabeth. *Themes from Web Talk, 2000.* Framingham, MA: IDC, 2000.

Frost & Sullivan. *U.S. IP Cable Telephony Market,* #6055-61. San Antonio, TX: Frost & Sullivan, 2001.

Frost & Sullivan, *Voice Over Internet Protocol Services Market Forecast Update,* #7401-61. San Antonio, TX: Frost & Sullivan, 2001.

Frost & Sullivan. *VoIP Equipment Subscription: Continuous Monitoring of Equipment Shipments and Market Developments,* #7396-61. San Antonio, TX: Frost & Sullivan, 2001.

Frost & Sullivan. *World Voice Portals Services Market,* #7912-65. San Antonio, TX: Frost & Sullivan, 2001.

iLocus.com. *Global Telephony Market 2000/01.* 2000.

InfoTech. *Professional Services for Converged Networks and Applications: Analysis of Leading Providers, June 2001.* New Jersey: InfoTech, 2001.

International Telecommunications Union. *ITU Report on Internet Telephony, 2001.* Geneva: International Telecommunications Union, 2000.

Jonas, Howard. *On a Roll: From Hot Dog Buns to High Tech Millions.* New York: Viking, 1998.

McCormick, Fritz. *Consumer Market Convergence, Report 17, Vol. 12.* Boston, MA: The Yankee Group, September 2000.

Morgan Stanley Dean Witter. *IP Telephony: Leveraging the Cable Network to Profitability in Voice.* February 14, 2001.

Standard Media International & Forrestor, LP. *Adopting the Broadband Future.* Net Insights, 2001.

Winther, Mark. *ITU Web Talk 2000: Market Forecast and Analysis.* Framingham, MA: IDC, 2000.

# Index

Accenture, 135, 137, 143
access charges levied by local
    access providers, 76
accessibility as an attribute of
    VoIP, 81
acquisitions and mergers
    2000, 54–55
    2001, 56
    2002, 56
    Adir, 42, 44
    AOL and Time Warner, 57
    cable telephony, IP, 121–124
    Comcast and AT&T Broad-
        band, 57
    Cox Communications/AT&T/
        Comcast, 124
    distribution and content
        companies, *xvi*
    IDT Telecom, 20, 21
    leading companies in move
        to convergence, 131
    TCI and AT&T, 57, 59
    Voice Over IP solutions, 14
ADC, 117, 118
Adelphia, 125
Adir, 13–14, 26–29, 56
    *see also* selling the vision of
        convergence
advanced messaging, 98, 99

advertising, *xv*
    *see also* free business model
        depending on advertising
        revenue as capital source
Africa, 86
Aibinder, Joseph, on conver-
    gence, 65
Alcatel, 50, 132, 134, 137–139,
    146, 148
Allied Business Intelligence,
    123
Analog Devices, 54
angel investors, 57
AOL, 22, 57, 148
AOL/Time Warner, 119
Armstrong, Michael
    cable IP telephony, develop-
        ing, 124
    value to customers, bringing,
        53
Arris Interactive, 117, 118
Asia, 83, 149
AT&T, 17–22, 50, 53, 57, 72, 92,
    122, 133
AT&T Broadband, 57, 122, 125
AT&T Comcast Corporation,
    114, 121
AT&T Solutions, 135
audioconferencing, 100–103
Audiotalk, 57

Auletta, Ken, on John Malone, 19
availability as an attribute of VoIP, 82
Avaya, 133, 134–135, 139–143

Balter, Howie, 16, 23, 24, 37
bandwidth, efficient use of, 62
Bell Labs, 33
Berkshire Hathaway, 59
best-in-breed solutions, 135
big deal, willingness to do the, 39–40
Bolivia, 149
Bordoli, Robin, on creating economic value, 127
brand recognition and strategic partnering/acquisition, 44
British Telecom, 86
Broadband network, 4, 84–85, 115–116, 123–124
*see also* cable telephony, IP
Buffett, Warren, 59
bundles, customized service, 95, 120–121, 132
business model focused solely around the cheap factor, 77
business models/platforms that convergence stimulates
convergence services as a subset of IP telephony, 132–133
metrics, establishment of, 133–136
partnerships/acquisitions and mergers, 93–94, 108, 138
professional services as a separate profit center, 131–132

CableLabs, 117
cable modem termination systems (CMTS), 117, 118

CableOne, 125
cable telephony, IP
broadband, 115–116, 123–124
business models/strategies/profitability, 124–128
convergence, great opportunity for, 6, 12
economic value of convergence, 126–127
growth in, 114
IP to cable, bringing, 116–117
multiple systems operators, leading, 125
overview, 113
primary service, making it a, 120–123
range of services, 113–114
rethinking/rexamining the industry, 11
selling, 118–120
standards for, 117–118
statistics on, 115
TCI sold to AT&T, 57, 59
trials, VoIP, 125–126
Cablevision, 114, 125
Cable & Wireless, 49–50, 149
callback technology, 16, 17–18
calling plans, customers flip-flopping between, 96
call routing solutions, 42
call waiting, Internet, 99–100
C-Cor.net, 56
Chambers, John, 51, 145
Charter Communications, 118, 125
Chile, 149
China, 68, 72
China Telecom, 149
circuit-switched technology, 74–75

Cisco, 50, 57
  acquisitions and mergers, 54,
    56
  Adir and, relationship be-
    tween, 80, 138
  Cox Communications, rela-
    tionship between, 122
  Customer Advocacy Group,
    137
  demand, convergence ser-
    vices on, 133
  equipment sales to Internet-
    based companies, 139
  leader in convergent services,
    144–146
  Net2Phone and, relationship
    between, 28
  partnerships, 143
  Professional Services Partner
    program, 136–137
  seamless integration of VoIP,
    51–52
  service providers targeted, 5
  Specialized Channel Partner
    program, 136–137
  subsidiary companies, 132
  success, recipe for, 134
Click-to-Talk, 61
cohesiveness, operational, 35
collaboration, 32, 38–39
Comcast, 53, 57, 122, 124, 125
ComMatch, 122
communicate, convergence
    changing way we, *xiii, xiv*,
    2–3, 48, 81–82, 98
community-enabled services
    that users can enable/dis-
    able, 12
community structure, idea of
    talking in a, 11
Compagnie Génerale d'Elec-
    tricité, 146

Compaq, 137
compassion, managing with a
    spirit of, 38
*Competing for the Future*
    (Hamel & Prahalad), 33
competition among telecom-
    munications service pro-
    viders, 95–96
Competitiveness Council, 18
ConferenceCenter products,
    1–2
connectivity as goal of conver-
    gence, advanced, *xiv*, 8
connotation and communica-
    tion, 3
consolidation, *see* acquisitions
    and mergers
consulting services, 135, 137
consumer services, adding
    voice to, 63–67
    *see also* services, convergent
content and distribution com-
    panies, acquisitions/merg-
    ers between, *xvi*
conveniences, consumer hun-
    ger for media-rich content
    and online, 64
convergence
  broadband network, 4
  cable market, 6, 12
  changes how we communi-
    cate, *xiii, xiv*, 48, 81–82, 98,
    151
ConferenceCenter products,
    1–2
  defining terms, *xiii*, 3
  enabling, 7–10
  financial industry, 12–13
  goal of, widespread connec-
    tivity as, *xiv*
  human voice to the customer
    experience, adding the,
    *xiv–xv*

ConferenceCenter products
(*continued*)
  intelligence, convergence
    representing a melding of,
    31
  interoperability, 5–6
  IP networks as backbone of,
    *xiv*
  live-person access not repre-
    sentative of full spectrum
    of, 91–92
  richer and more meaningful
    communication, 2–3
  self-provisioning, 6
  service types born of, pre-
    dicting, 4–5
  softswitch, 5
  true, in search of, 3–7
  unstoppable path, 63
  where will it take us, 10–12
  *see also individual subject
    headings*
Convergent Networks, 118
CoreExpress, 103
corporations that adopt IP tele-
    phony, advantages/bene-
    fits for, 61–63, 86, 97–98
CosmoCom, 58
cost-effectiveness of IP tele-
    phony, 61–63, 77, 82, 96,
    117
costs of converting PSTN/en-
    terprise networks, 62–63,
    78, 80, 116
Cox Communications, 114, 121,
    124, 125
credibility and strategic rela-
    tionships, 43
culture, organizational, 35–40
customer development and
    strategic partnering/acqui-
    sition, 44

customer feedback, 34, 134, 135
customer relationship manage-
    ment (CRM), 64, 94, 107,
    141
customer retention, 107
customer satisfaction, 134, 135
customer service/support, 134,
    145–146
customized service bundles, 95,
    108, 120–121, 132

Datacraft, 138
Dataflex, 54
Data Over Cable System Inter-
    face Specifications (DOC-
    SIS), 117–118, 122
dependability, 2
deregulation, 82–83, 95–96,
    119–120
design team, 33–34
Deutsche Telekom, 72
developing nations, 67–68
dialers that constantly dial into
    gateways through PSTN in-
    terface, 9
Dialpad.com, 58
differentiation in approaches/
    products/services, 90
digital convergence, 4
direction change, ability to
    handle, 41
Disney, 115, 119
distribution and content com-
    panies, acquisitions/merg-
    ers between, *xvi*
distribution channels, 134
Dow Chemical, 65
DTVN Holdings, 103

EDS, 98, 135, 137
eMarketer, 123
emotional health affected by
    communication quality, 2

EmpowerTel Networks, 58
enterprise segment *vs.* con-
    sumer market, growth and,
    109
enterprise solutions, 42
entertainment industry, *xv*,
    115–116
equipment, networking, 134,
    136, 140
Ericcson, 50, 86
e-smith, Inc., 122–123
Europe, Western, 83
European Telecommunications
    Standards Institute (ETSI),
    77
Euslin, Tom, 148
Eyak, 58

failproof systems, 33
family, treating employees as,
    38
Federal Communications Com-
    mission (FCC), 18, 121
feedback, customer, 34, 134,
    135
FIFA World Cup (2002), 141
financial industry, *xv*, 12–13,
    57–59, 92, 95, 142
flexibility, 32, 48, 96
Forbes, 18
Fox, 115
free business model depending
    on advertising revenue as
    capital source, 92, 93, 96,
    97, 108, 109
Frost & Sullivan, 94–95, 101,
    117, 126
functionality, 2, 61, 67, 75
fundraising, 42–43

Gallery IP, 122
Gartner Consulting, 127

General Bandwidth, 58
General Electric, 146
generosity, managing with a
    spirit of, 38
Genuity, 56, 148
Getronics, 138
Glowpoint, 103
Goldberg, Jeff, 23, 33
growth and enterprise segment
    *vs.* consumer market, 109

Hamel, Gary, 33
hat trick model, 121
health care industry, *xv*
HearMe, 57, 101
Hewlett Packard, 137, 143
hiring practices, 34–35
home, VoIP at, 85
Homeworx solution, 118
human voice to the customer
    experience, adding the,
    *xiv–xv*, 63–64
    *see also* services, convergent;
    voice *listings; individual
    subject headings*
humility, 38–39, 41

iBasis, 50, 54, 92
IBM, 22, 43, 92
IBM's Global Services, 98, 135–
    137, 143
ICServiceWorks, 118
IDC, 57
IDT Telecom, 7
    AT&T, deal making with,
        17–22
    callback carrier to a carrier's
        carrier, 22
    callback technology, 16
    infrastructure and retail rela-
        tionships for communica-
        tions, 15

IDT Telecom (*continued*)
  Knoller, Marc, 15–16
  Malone (John) invests in, 19–22
  Net2Phone's ongoing relationship with, 28–29
  professionals involved, many talented, 16–17
  *On a Roll: From Hot Dog Buns to High Tech Millions* (Jonas), 15
  timeline, 18–19
Indonesia, 86
industry's perspective on convergence
  broadband network, 84–85
  challenges/solutions to adopting IP telephony, 78, 80
  corporate interest in IP telephony, 86
  deconstructing VoIP, 80–81
  global IP telephony, evolution, 71–74
  IP networks, explaining, 74–76
  market drivers boosting popularity of VoIP, 82–84, 95–97
  paradigm shift in communications, 81–82
  PC-to-Phone, 71–72
  regulations governing IP telephony, 76–77
  standards for IP telephony, 77–79
  summary/conclusions, 86–87
  wireless technology, 85–86
information-foisting technologies, 107
innovation, 42, 127

insecurity, consumer, 64
Insight Communications, 125
instantaneous service with a personal touch, consumer expectation of, 64
instant messaging, *xv*, 61
institutional investment, 57–59
integrated network management solutions, 61, 62
Intel, 50, 52
Intel Converged Communications Platform (ICCP), 52
intelligence, convergence representing a melding of, 31
intelligent software tools, 8
international interest in IP telephony, 49, 67–68, 71–74
International Telecommunications Union (ITU), 68, 77, 79
Internet, software creation process changed by the, 44
Internet call waiting, 99–100
Internet Computer Systems, 21
Internet Engineering Task Force (IETF), 77–79
Internet Exchange Architecture (IXA), 52
Internet Protocol (IP) networks, *xii–xiv*, 7, 8, 47–48, 74–76
  *see also individual subject headings*
Internet service providers (ISPs), 121
interoperability as an attribute of VoIP, 5–6, 52, 82, 117
interpretation and communication, 3
investment bankers, 43
IP, *see* Internet Protocol networks
IPO (initial public offering) for Net2Phone, 23–26

IP Unity, 122
ipVerse, 59
ITXC (Internet Telephony Exchange Carrier), 52, 55, 148–150

Japan, 141
JFAX.com., 55
jitter effect, 80
Jonas, Howard, 7, 37
  Malone (John), relationship with, 17, 19–20, 22
  *On a Roll: From Hot Dog Buns to High Tech Millions*, 15, 17
  vision of IP telephony, articulating the, 32
Juniper, 140

Kagnoff, Moshe, 16
Katzenbach, Jon (*The Wisdom of Teams*), 33
killer applications, 48
kindness, managing with a spirit of, 38
Knoller, Marc, 15–16
Korea, 141
KPMG, 136, 137, 143

latency, 80
layoffs, 39, 145
leaders in convergent services
  Avaya, 140–142
  cable telephony, IP, 125
  Cisco, 144–146
  companies to watch, 146, 148–150
  comparison (financial) of leading convergence companies, 147
  overview, 138–140

shift of market dominance, 138–139
  3Com, 142–144
leading a visionary company, 40–41
legacy systems, 96
Legg Mason, 59
Level 3 Communications, 56, 59
Levy, Jonathan, 16
liberalization, telecommunications, 83
Liberty Media, 19, 20, 22, 57
Lichtenstein, Motti, 16
lifeline marketplace and IP cable telephony, 120–123
live-person access not representative of full spectrum of convergence, 91–92
Longleaf Partners, 59
Lucent, 50, 52, 141

Malone, John
  Jonas (Howard), relationship with, 17, 19–20, 22
  TCI, sale of, 57, 59, 122
market's perspective on convergence
  advantages/benefits for corporations that adopt IP telephony, 61–63
  Cisco, 51–52
  consumer services, adding voice to, 63–67
  emergent themes, two, 48
  financial industry, 57–59
  Intel, 52
  international interest in IP telephony, 49, 67–68
  investment in race to develop services and technologies, 49–50
  joint ventures/alliances/acquisitions, 52–56

market's perspective on convergence (*continued*)
minor players managing lucrative businesses, 51
players: companies to watch, 50–52
revenue projections, 60–61
summary/conclusions, 68–69
value for investors, adding greater, 13–14
VoIP, market forecasts for, 66–67
McCormick, Rob, on network technology, 12–13
McGregor, Douglas, on self-motivated employees, 36
McIntosh, Dan, 18
Mediacon, 125
Media Gateway Control Protocol (MGCP), 77, 78
media gateways (MGs), 75–76
media industry, *xv*, 115–116
MediaNet, 72
MediaOne, 122
MediaRing, 50
mediator, Voice Over IP solutions as the great, 48
mental health affected by communication quality, 2
mergers, *see* acquisitions and mergers
Merrill Lynch, 12
metrics used to help outperform the competition, 131, 133–136
MGM, 115
Microsoft, 50
Middle East, 149
Mind CTI, 138
Miners, 10
minor players managing lucrative businesses, 51

Mitel, 122–123
Mobius Venture Capital, 127
moderation, 37–38
monitoring capabilities, 9–10, 27
motivation, self-, 36, 41
Motorola, 118, 122, 138
movie industry, 115–116
multiple systems operators (MSOs), 114–115, 125
*see also* cable telephony, IP

National Cable & Telecommunications Association (NCTA), 114, 118
National Convergence Alliance, 5
NCR, 137
Nepal, 67
Net2Phone
AT&T invests in, 20, 53
callback to full-scale carrier, 22–23
Cisco and, relationship between, 28
Click-to-Talk, 61
creation of, *xv–xvi*
future solutions, developing, 50–51
highlights, 25
IDT and Liberty Media purchase, 22
IDT Telecom's ongoing relationship with, 28–29
Internet telephony market, winning two-thirds of, 23
interplay among huge corporate investments, 57
IPO (initial public offering), 23–26
Netscape, agreement with, 39
partnerships, 26–28

services that are profit centers of IP telephony market, 92

tool development for future communication services/applications, 7–8

Voice Over IP solutions created by, 23

Voxis, 8–9

*see also individual subject headings*

Netscape, 39

Netsmart, 138

NetSpeak, 13, 14, 42, 44, 80

Net Voice, 55

network convergence, 4

network management, 104

Nextira, 137

Nextwave, 1–2

Nokia, 86

Nordstrom's, *xv*

Norstan, 138

Nortel, 50, 86, 122, 132, 134, 137–139

Nortel's Internal Global Professional Services group, 137

Nortel's Premier Service Provider (PSP), 137

Old School approach towards technology, 90

*On a Roll: From Hot Dog Buns to High Tech Millions* (Jonas), 15, 17

Onebox.com, 57

open environment, 37

optimum level, ensuring that company/employees are operating at, 40

Optus, 149

Orion Telekom BV, 21

outsourcing Web services from

other service providers, 109, 112

Ovum, 123

Pace Micro Technology, 55

Pacific Rim countries, 83, 86, 149

packet transmissions, *xiv*, 8, 74–75

Paramount, 115

partnerships

business models/platform that convergence stimulates, 136–138

cable telephony, IP, 119–123

IBM's Global Services, 135

ITXC, 149

leaders in convergent services, 143

leading companies in move to convergence, 131

manufactures and service providers, 136

metrics, the use of, 134

Net2Phone, 26–28

Netscape and Net2Phone, 39

Seibel Systems, 94

selling the vision of convergence, 42–45

value-added resellers and manufactures, 136

Paulson, Ed, on VoIP as future of Cisco, 51

PCIX, 21

PC-to-Phone, 71–73

Phone.com, 57

PhoneCube, 101

Pingtel, 59

point-of-sale experiences, 107

Polycom, 55

Prahalad, C. K., 33

prepaid calling market, 22, 72

pricing issues
   business models deployed by
      service providers, 94
   customized service bundles,
      121
   developing nations, 67–68
   selling the vision of conver-
      gence, 32, 33
   services offered, pricing strat-
      egy commensurate with
      value of, 93, 97
   value for customers offering
      greater flexibility for prices,
      96
   videoconferencing, 103
primary service, making IP
   cable telephony a, 120–
   123, 126
productivity increased by
   adopting IP telephony solutions, 62
product line extensions and
   strategic partnering/acqui-
   sition, 44
profits/revenues/sales
   audio-/videoconferencing,
      102–103
   business models/platform
      that convergence stimu-
      lates, 131–132
   cable telephony, IP, 120, 126,
      128
   Cisco, 144–146
   consumer voice Web ser-
      vices, 111
   corporate expenditures for
      convergence services/
      equipment, 130
   global IP network, 50
   IP telephony and voice ser-
      vices, 13
   ITXC, 149–150

leading companies in move
   to convergence, 129
Old School approach, 90
outsourcing Web services
   from other service providers, 112
projections for IP telephony,
   60–61
services that are profit centers of IP telephony market, 92
softswitch market, 5
Voice Over IP solutions, 6–7
voice portal services market,
   110
PSTN, see public switch telephone networks
PT-I Debit Card Business, 21
public awareness about voice
   portals, 105
public switch telephone networks (PSTNs), 5, 7, 9, 47,
   67
publishing, xv
Pulver, Jeff, on SIP, 78
Pulver.com, 78

quality of service (QoS)
   challenge to adopting IP tele-
      phony, 78, 80
   criticism concerning, 73
   Data Over Cable System In-
      terface Specifications, 117
   emotional/mental health af-
      fected by communication
      quality, 2
   Internet Protocol networks,
      74–75
   KPMG, 136
   metrics, the use of, 134
   voice portals, 104
Quayle, Dan, 18

Rapid 5 Networks, 58
real-time application on IP, Voice Over IP solutions as first, 10
Regional Bell Operating Company (RBOC), 20, 22, 121, 149
regulations governing IP telephony, 68, 76–77
reinvention, 41, 90
relationship value, strategic relationships and, 43
reliability
    as an attribute of VoIP, 82
    challenge to adopting IP telephony, 80
    corporate setting, adopting IP telephony in, 62
    criticism concerning, 73
    Net2Phone and IDT Telecom, relationship between, 29
    paradigm shift in communications, 82
    voice portals, 104, 105
Rendall, David, on advanced information services economy, 127
repairing problems, Voice Over IP solutions and, 8
research and design (R&D), 105
retail services, *xv*
rethinking/rexamining the industry, 11
revenue projections for IP telephony, 60–61
    *see also* profits/revenues/ sales
Riechel, Gary, 43
right place for the right person, finding the, 35–36
risk taking, 32
Rochwarger, Geoff, 16

Rock Enterprises, 21
Rogers Cantel, 86
role models and strategic relationships, 43
Rothberg, Mordy, 24, 27
    on convergence, 5–6

SAIC, 135, 137, 138
sales, 107
    *see also* profits/revenues/ sales
Sarnoff, David, 113
Savvis Communications, 12–13
SBC, 133, 137
scalable technology as an attribute of VoIP, 32, 82, 116, 117
Seibel Systems, 94
self-assessment, 41
self-healing capability, 10
self-motivated employees, 36, 41
self-provisioning, 6
selling the vision of convergence
    big deal, willingness to do the, 39–40
    cable telephony, IP, 118–120
    communicating the vision, 34
    complex requirements of running voice/video over one homogenous network, 32
    culture, organizational, 35–40
    design team, 33–34
    educating the market as convergent services continue to evolve, 32
    failproof systems, 33
    humility, show, 38–39
    image change from PC-to-phone telco company, 32

selling the vision of convergence (*continued*)
  innovation, 42
  Jonas (Howard) articulating vision of IP telephony, 32
  leading a visionary company, 40–41
  moderation, 37–38
  participant, everyone is a, 34–35
  partnerships and deals, 42–45
  pricing, focus on adding services more than, 33
  right place for the right person, finding the, 35–36
  scalable technology, 32
  teamwork, 31, 33, 36–37
service providers, 5, 93–96, 107–108
  *see also individual subject headings*
services, convergent
  advanced messaging and residential call management, 99–100
  audio-/videoconferencing, 100–103
  business models deployed by service providers, 93–94
  business models/platform that convergence stimulates, 131–133
  community-enabled services that users can enable/disable, 12
  conveniences, consumer hunger for media-rich content and online, 64
  corporate users, people at home enjoying same services as, 4

customized service bundles, 95, 108, 120–121, 132
educating the market as convergent services continue to evolve, 32
growth in, 129, 130
instantaneous service with a personal touch, consumer expectation of, 64
investment in race to develop services and technologies, 49–50
leading companies in move to convergence, 131
predicting types of services that will be born of convergence, 4–5
pricing strategies commensurate with value of services offered, 93, 97
profit centers of the IP telephony market, 92
selling the vision of convergence, 33
service providers, advantages for, 107–108
subset of IP telephony, 132–133
trials of convergent services in select markets, 42
Voice Over IP solutions as primary driver, 65–67
voice portals, 104–112
Shoreline Networks, 59
Siemens, 132, 133, 139, 143, 146
SIP (Session Initial Protocol), 78
Slasky, Ilan, 23, 24
Sobel, Cliff, 23
Softbank, 24, 43
Softbank Venture Capital, 28
softswitch technology, 5, 74–75
software creation process, the Internet changing the, 44

Son, Masayoshi, 24
Sonera, 72
Sonus Networks, 55
Sony, 115
speech recognition technologies, 95, 104, 105
speed, 32
Sprint, 103
SS8 Networks, 56, 59
stand-alone service, 120
standards for IP telephony, 77–79, 117–118
strategic relationships, 42–45, 131, 138
    see also partnerships
streamers, 9–10
Sun Microsystems, 148
suspicious behavior targeted by Voice Over IP solutions, 8
SYSCOM, 138
Systems integrators, 135, 136
systems integrators, 134

target markets, 93
Taylorism, 36
TCI, 19, 22, 57, 59, 122
teamwork, 31, 33, 35, 36–37
technology and timing, success and the confluence of, 5
teenage lines, 67
Telcopoint, 101
Telecom Finland, 72
Telecom Italia Mobile, 86
Telecommunications Act of 1996, 76, 119–120
Telenor AS, 86
television, 113
Tellabs, 117
Telstra, 149
text-to-speech technologies, 104, 105
Thomson Multimedia, 122

3Com, 5
3Cube, 101
3Com, 50, 132, 134, 138, 139, 142–144
3Com's Convergence Leadership Alliance Program, 137
3G.IP, 86
Time Warner, 57, 121, 122, 125
timing and technology, success and the confluence of, 5
training, 62–63, 134, 136
transport capability of the network, monitoring the, 9
trend data from multiple places/multiple gateways, comparing, 10
trials of convergent services in select markets, 42, 125–126

Ubiquity, 58
unified function devices, 8
unified messaging, 7, 99–100
Unisphere Networks, 55
Unisys, 137
Universal Pictures, 115
universal service fund, mandatory contributions to the, 76
unstoppable path, convergence is on an, 63

value-added resellers (VARs), 136
value-based management thinking, 36
value for investors, adding greater, 13–14, 40, 43, 53
venture capital, 42, 57
Veracast, 1–2
Verizon, 133
viability as an attribute of VoIP, 81

Viacom, 119
videoconferencing, 98, 100–103
vision of convergence, *see* selling the vision of convergence
VocalData, 59
Voice Over IP (VoIP) solutions
    acquisitions/mergers, 14
    financial industry, 12–13
    forecasts for, market, 66–67
    goal of, widespread connectivity as, 8
    at home, 85
    Internet Protocol networks combined with, *xiii–xiv*
    mediator, the great, 48
    minutes/capital investment/revenue as ways to measure potential of, 8, 84
    Net2Phone, creation of, *xv–xvi*, 23
    profits/revenues/sales, 6–7
    real-time application, 10
    repairing problems, 8
    selling the vision of convergence, 40–41
    services, primary driver in development of convergent, 65–67
    suspicious behavior, targeting, 8
    traffic carried over, 8, 84

Voxis, 8–10
*see also individual subject headings*
voice portals, 7, 104–112
Voice XML, 95
VoIP, *see* Voice Over IP solutions
VoIP Telecom, 55
Vonage, 57
Voxis, 8–10
VxTel, 52

Wall Street, 12–13, 57–59
Walt Disney Company, 115, 119
Warner Studios, 115
weeding-out phase, communications industry in a, 56
Winkler, Joshua, 17
wireless technology, 7, 11, 85–86
Wire One, 103
*Wisdom of Teams, The* (Katzenbach), 33
Woodman, Allistair, 28

XoIP (anything over IP), 73

Yahoo!, 22, 148

ZAO Investelectrosvyaz, 21
Zhone Technologies, 55, 56
Zimbabwe, 149